Developing Literacy
TEXT LEVEL

TEXT-LEVEL ACTIVITIES FOR THE LITERACY HOUR

year

6

Ray Barker

Christine Moorcroft

A & C BLACK

Reprinted 2001 (twice), 2002 (twice)
Published 2000 by
A&C Black Publishers Limited
37 Soho Square, London W1D 3QZ
www.acblack.com

ISBN 0-7136-5321-3

Acknowledgements
The authors and publishers are grateful for permission to reproduce the following:
page 15: Three clerihews by Edmund Clerihew Bentley from *Clerihews Complete* (T Werner Laurie Ltd)
by permission of Bella Jones; page 30: 'The Wind' by James Stephens by permission of the Society of Authors as the
literary representatives of the Estate of James Stephens.

Every effort has been made to trace copyright holders and to obtain their permission for use of copyright material.
The authors and publishers would be pleased to rectify in future editions any error or omission.

The authors and publishers would like to thank the following teachers
for their advice in producing this series of books:

Jane Beynon; Hardip Channa; Ann Hart; Lydia Hunt;
Rita Leader; Madeleine Madden; Helen Mason; Kim Pérez;
Joanne Turpin; Fleur Whatley

A CIP catalogue record for this book is
available from the British Library.

A & C Black uses paper produced with elemental chlorine-free pulp,
harvested from managed sustainable forests.

Printed in Great Britain by
St Edmundsbury Press Ltd, Bury St Edmunds, Suffolk.

Contents

Introduction

Developing Literacy: Text Level supports the teaching of reading and writing by providing a series of activities to develop children's ability to recognise and appreciate the different genres, styles and purposes of text. **Year 6** encourages them to read texts from a variety of genres (both non-fiction and fiction), looking at narrative perspective, point of view and the way writing is structured. It develops their enjoyment of stories and poetry and provides frameworks which help them to compose their own. It also provides structures on which they can base their non-fiction writing for particular purposes.

The activities are designed to be carried out in the time allocated to independent work during the Literacy Hour. They support the objectives of the National Literacy Strategy *Framework for Teaching* at text level and they incorporate strategies which encourage independent learning – for example, ways in which children can check their own work or that of a partner.

The focus of the activities in **Year 6** is to build upon and revise the work of earlier years. Investigation is therefore given greater emphasis in order to revisit topics already covered, but at a higher level, and to encourage independent thought.

Year 6 helps children to:
- evaluate the work of individual writers;
- comment critically on the overall impact of a work;
- explore narrative order and plan stories for a variety of genres;
- write summaries and reviews;
- look closely at a variety of poetic forms and write their own poems;
- secure an understanding of the language features of different non-fiction texts;
- recognise the ways in which texts are written for particular readers;
- make notes in a variety of ways and summarise ideas;
- edit and review their own writing.

Year 6 also develops the children's ability to:
- identify features of non-fiction texts;
- write in a variety of forms, such as explanations, instructions and non-chronological reports;
- experiment with, and adapt, different poetic forms;
- understand how descriptive and figurative language can create moods and feelings;
- select the appropriate style and form to suit a specific purpose and audience, drawing on their knowledge.

Extension

Most of the activity sheets end with a challenge (**Now try this!**) which reinforces and extends the children's learning and provides the teacher with an opportunity for assessment. These more challenging activities might be appropriate for only a few children; it is not expected that the whole class should complete them. On some pages there is space for the children to complete the extension activities, but for others they will need a notebook or separate sheet of paper.

Organisation

Few resources are needed besides scissors, glue, a variety of text-types (for example, newspapers and leaflets), word-banks and a range of dictionaries. The activities have all been designed for use in conjunction with readily available texts of your choice.

To help teachers to select appropriate learning experiences for their pupils, the activities are grouped into sections within the book. The pages need not be presented in the order in which they appear, unless otherwise stated.

Teachers' notes

Brief notes are provided at the bottom of most pages. They give ideas and suggestions for making the most of the activity sheet. They sometimes make suggestions for the whole class introduction, the plenary session or follow-up work using an adapted version of the activity sheet.

Structure of the Literacy Hour

The following chart shows an example of the way in which an activity from this book can be used to achieve the required organisation of the Literacy Hour.

Points of view (page 9)

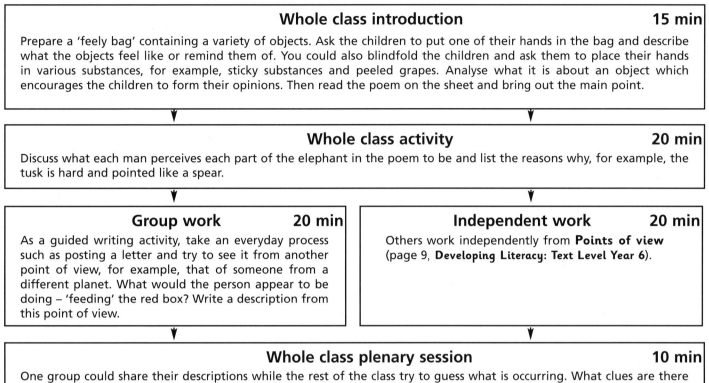

Whole class introduction   **15 min**

Prepare a 'feely bag' containing a variety of objects. Ask the children to put one of their hands in the bag and describe what the objects feel like or remind them of. You could also blindfold the children and ask them to place their hands in various substances, for example, sticky substances and peeled grapes. Analyse what it is about an object which encourages the children to form their opinions. Then read the poem on the sheet and bring out the main point.

Whole class activity   **20 min**

Discuss what each man perceives each part of the elephant in the poem to be and list the reasons why, for example, the tusk is hard and pointed like a spear.

Group work   **20 min**

As a guided writing activity, take an everyday process such as posting a letter and try to see it from another point of view, for example, that of someone from a different planet. What would the person appear to be doing – 'feeding' the red box? Write a description from this point of view.

Independent work   **20 min**

Others work independently from **Points of view** (page 9, **Developing Literacy: Text Level Year 6**).

Whole class plenary session   **10 min**

One group could share their descriptions while the rest of the class try to guess what is occurring. What clues are there which may help them? The other group could say what other parts of the elephant might be like. Finish by reading the two verses of the poem again.

Using the activity sheets

Fiction and poetry: reading comprehension

Investigate: Points of view (page 9) enables the children to consider the many different ways in which the same object can be perceived. This should be developed into the children's reading. Which books are written from a particular point of view? What happens if you switch the point of view to that of another character?

Investigate: A personal response (page 10) and **Investigate: Authors and their work** (page 11) provide formats which can be used with any texts. The sheets allow the children to research and to contribute constructively to discussion, with evidence to back their arguments.

Investigate: Time (page 12) provides a checklist for the children to consider the impact of time in fiction. This links with later work on 'flashback' and story structure and can be a focus for the discussion of the value of certain story endings, such as 'and then I woke up' or 'it was all a dream'.

Investigate: Sentence order (page 13) links with sentence-level work: to be in control of their writing it is important for the children to start to analyse how individual paragraphs are structured in writing. The original paragraph is:

In a sporting contest, a referee or umpire makes sure that players keep to the rules and decides who is the winner. He or she should be fair to all, know all the rules and give decisions at once. Players must accept his or her decision without question. If you argue with the referee, it is 'bad sportsmanship'. A footballer, for example, risks being sent off the pitch for arguing with the referee.

Rhythm: sea shanties (page 14) examines sea-shanties as an example of rhythm in context. **Rhyme: clerihews** (page 15) takes the clerihew form as an example of rhyme. These are both 'miniature' forms but they will enable the children to be able to write in the style and be successful. The original clerihew by Bentley was:

Sir Christopher Wren
Said, 'I am going to dine with some men.
'If anyone calls
'Say I am designing St Paul's.'

Investigate: Figurative language (page 16) encourages children to investigate the use of simile, metaphor and personification and to incorporate some of these in their own structured creative writing.

Playing with language (page 17) shows how poets manipulate words for their sound quality and humour. This activity links with **Investigate: Ambiguity** (page 18), which shows how the English language is rich in meaning and that to 'mean what you say' is not always 'to say what you mean'. Again the focus is on fun.

Lewis Carroll was the master of nonsense verse; **Nonsense verse** (page 19) encourages the children to use their imagination and manipulate language in the same way as Carroll. A contrasting approach to responding to verse is found in **Moods and feelings in poetry** (page 20) which gives the children the opportunity to respond freely to the sensuous nature of poetic language: the idea is that poets choose specific words to create a specific mood or feeling.

Characters (page 21) concentrates on characters and their purpose in a book. The children should become aware that characters are placed in a narrative with a function: for example, to move the story forward in some way.

Suspense (page 22) deals with suspense and how writers manipulate the feelings of their readers.

Compare and contrast (page 23) and **Investigate: Writing about books** (page 24) are generic formats which help the children to compare works by the same author and works by a variety of authors. Any part of these sheets could be chosen as an area of research, and it is not necessary to complete the information for all the categories.

Fiction and poetry: writing composition

A story with a moral (page 25) looks at how an ancient story-line can be used to tell a 'modern story'. It focuses on the *theme* of the text rather than the content. **Analyse a story** (page 26) takes this one stage further, to consider how authors use characters and situations to develop a variety of plot lines.

Investigate: Summarising (page 27) links with sentence-level work but asks the children to consider the main idea of a text and how they can best communicate this in as few words as possible.

In **Write a story as a playscript** (page 28) children are asked to re-write a narrative text as a playscript, following the dramatic conventions.

Investigate: 'Strong' verbs (page 29) and **Investigate: Personification** (page 30) both require the children to respond to a poetry text. While the first looks closely at the power of language in communicating an idea, and what happens if you adapt this, the second looks at how an image can be created by using figures of speech. These activities require the children to examine the words on the page, experiment with language and effects and make judgements about what they have created.

Investigate: Flashbacks (page 31) looks at how time can be manipulated. The children are asked to investigate and to experiment with the effects of changing the time-line of a story.

Investigate: Parody (page 32) uses what the children know of a form to be able to manipulate this to their own ends. Lewis Carroll's version of 'Twinkle, twinkle…' is:

Twinkle, twinkle little bat!
How I wonder what you're at!
Up above the world you fly,
Like a tea-tray in the sky.

Shop signs (page 33) is an amusing illustration about how language can easily be manipulated for effect.

How to annotate a passage (page 34) practises a valuable skill when looking for aspects of narrative and the author's intentions in a passage. This also links with the work of previous years on note-taking.

The next three sheets in this section are all generic formats which help the children to respond personally to books in different ways, from the long-term communication of their reading habits in **A reading journal** (page 35), to the summarising of the impact of a book in **Investigate: 'Blurb'** (page 36) and to the writing of a more traditional account of a text in **A book review** (page 37).

In **Write a riddle** (page 38), the children are given the opportunity to write a poem sequence using the traditional riddle format. Again, this is a simple format, but it requires the children to be able to exercise a great deal of control over their writing. The form is 'small scale' but a successful riddle is very difficult to write.

The first riddle contains clues such as 'eyes' and 'skin'. The answer is a potato.
The answer to the second riddle is soap.
The answer to the third riddle is a glove.
The chair riddle could contain references to body parts (legs, arms, back) as well as human characteristics such as standing. You could link it to work on personification on page 30.

Non-fiction: reading comprehension

Investigate: Biographies (page 39) considers the use of point of view and the use of third person narration, whereas **Investigate: Autobiographies** (page 40) looks at first person narration techniques.

<u>Biography</u>: passages 1 and 3 contain features of biography – third person narration about the life of someone else. Examples of these features are the use of the word 'he', as well as the use of significant detail. Passages 2 and 4 use the first person ('I') so cannot be biographical.

<u>Autobiography</u>: passages 3 and 4 contain features of autobiography – first person narration about the person's life. Examples are the word 'I', and the use of significant, personal detail. Passages 1 and 2 use the third person, so cannot be autobiographical.

Investigate: Reports (page 41), **Investigate: Leaflets** (page 42), **Investigate: Journalism** (page 43), **Investigate: Non-chronological reports** (page 44) and **Investigate: Explanations** (page 45) all use a similar format to enable the children to extract from short texts the essence of these non-fiction text-types. This information can then be extended into their own writing and revised in class through shared reading.

Construct an argument (page 46) provides a format to help the children write down the stages by which arguments are constructed in order to be effective: for example, a sequence of linking points and appealing to the known views and feelings of the audience.

A balanced argument (page 47) provides the children with a list of the necessary 'argument words' which assist in the development of their thoughts, and will enable them to summarise both sides of an argument.

Investigate: Official language (page 48) helps the children to examine examples of this kind of 'formal' language and its characteristic features, and **Investigate: Impersonal language** (page 49) shows how technical and highly specific language needs to be used for certain kinds of description, and where it is inappropriate.

Retrieving information (page 50) shows how the labelling of a diagram is an effective way of extracting information, and **Skimming and scanning** (page 51) looks at the value of being familiar with both of these valuable techniques in note-taking.

Non-fiction: writing composition

Writing a biography (page 52) gives the children key questions with which to structure and write a biography.

Writing an autobiography (page 53) leads the children through the key moments of their lives so that they can structure and write their autobiographies.

The next three sheets provide 'fun' formats which will show the children how to consider characters from their reading in a variety of different ways while revising well-known styles: for example, **A character's CV** (page 54), **A character's school report** (page 55) and **A character's personal file** (page 56). These sheets focus on the skills of biographical and autobiographical writing, but *in role*.

Be a journalist (page 57) aims to help the children to develop a journalistic style. **Using the Internet** (page 58) helps them to use ICT to plan, revise and research their work. Using this technology is very exciting and motivating for most children but they need a great deal of structure to be able to make the most of the medium.

The remaining activities in this section seek to give a practical expression to the comprehension sheets of the previous section. They use the features which the children have identified in non-fiction text-types and they provide a stimulus to help the children to write in this form, for example: **Write effective arguments** (page 59) and **Write a balanced report** (page 60).

Investigate: Standard English (page 61) provides a passage from classic fiction so that the children can identify the purpose of using non-standard English. They should be reaching the conclusion that it is not necessarily 'wrong' but is used at its best to give a sense of character and of time and place. When the children investigate changing the language they should become aware of just how much has been removed of the power of the original.

Investigate: Impersonal writing (page 62) looks at the language of science. The correct versions of the two pieces of impersonal writing are:

<u>To demonstrate</u> water pressure.
First, a plastic bucket was taken.
Three holes were drilled in it – one near the rim, one in the centre and one near the base.
The holes were sealed with masking tape.
Then the bucket was filled with water.
When the tape was removed, the water sprayed out through the holes. From this it is possible to see where the pressure is greatest.

Growing crystals

First, heated water was poured over sugar in a pan and stirred with a spatula until no more sugar would dissolve.
This sugary liquid, called a solution, was placed in a beaker.
Then a sugar cube was tied with fine thread and suspended in the solution.
Crystals were seen to grow on the thread after a few days.

Investigate: Paragraphs (page 63) provides a logical structure and rationale behind a piece of writing and asks the children to provide the content.

Text-types (page 64) revises non-fiction text-types and why they are relevant to specific purposes. It demands a sophisticated response from the children in that they are investigating the demands of the audiences of each of the extracts. The answers are:

Text 1: Recount text – in this case a personal one.
Text 2: Instructional text. Look at the imperative verbs in the recipe.
Text 3: Information text.
Text 4: Persuasive text. It is obviously an advertisement and so aims to persuade the reader about something.

Glossary of terms used

ambiguity This occurs when a phrase or statement has more than one meaning or interpretation.
author The person who writes the text. See also **narrator.**
autobiography A life story of a person, written *by* that person. It is usually written in the first person.
biography A life story of someone written by another author. It is generally written in the third person.
chronology A sequence of events in time, from Cronos, the God of Time.
clerihew A comic poetic form invented by Edmund Clerihew Bentley. Each poem has four lines, starts with a name and rhymes in two couplets. The lines may be of any length.
discussion text A text which gives *all sides* of an issue. It can be written or spoken.
explanatory text A text which explains a process or answers a question.
figurative language Language which is not literal (factual), for example: simile and metaphor. Such language is used to create mood or atmosphere.
genre A specific type of writing or other medium of communication, for example: *legend, newspaper story* or *poem.*
instructional text A text which gives the reader information to be able to carry out some aim, for example: to make something or to reach a particular place. Instructions use the imperative (command) form of the verb.
literal language Language which is factual, as opposed to **figurative.**
metaphor A comparison, but stronger than a **simile.** Metaphors say something *is* something else, for example: *The road was a ribbon of moonlight.*
narrative A text which retells events or a story, often in chronological order.
narrator Whoever tells the story in the text; not necessarily the author.
non-chronological text Writing which is structured or organised with no reference to chronological order, for example: a report on a town organised in sub-headings such as 'population', 'location'.
parody An imitation of a text, making fun of the style, language or content of a text.
personification This is a form of metaphor in which some 'thing' is said to have human characteristics, for example: *The sun smiled down on us.*
playscript A text written to be performed. The format of a playscript is designed to make actors and directors interpret the text for performance, hence the inclusion of stage directions and clues for more effective performance.
recount A text (or part of a text) usually written in the past tense to re-tell for information or entertainment. It uses descriptive language and might include dialogue.
report A non-chronological text usually written in the present tense to describe or classify.
rhyme Words containing the same sound in their last syllables, for example: *go/slow, say/grey.*
scan To look at a text quickly, to locate key words and ideas.
skim To read a passage to gain an initial overview of the subject matter.

Points of view

We do not all view things in the same way.

- **Read these verses of a poem, in which two blind men are introduced to an elephant.**

The First approached the Elephant,
And happening to fall
Against his broad and sturdy side,
At once began to bawl:
'God bless me! but the Elephant
Is very like a wall!'

The Second, feeling of the tusk,
Cried, 'Ho! what have we here
So very round and smooth and sharp?
To me 'tis mighty clear
The wonder of an Elephant
Is very like a spear!'

FROM *The Blind Men and the Elephant* BY JOHN SAXE

- **Underline what each blind man thinks the elephant is.**

- **Explain how each man forms his opinion.**

Verse 1	Verse 2

- **What do these parts of an elephant remind you of?**

The trunk _____   The leg _____

The ear _____   The tail _____

Now try this!

- **Imagine you are an alien seeing objects on Earth for the first time (for example a postbox or a pushchair).**
- **Write what you think the objects might be, and why.**

Teachers' note To introduce this topic during shared reading, identify the narrator of different stories and discuss the viewpoint of the texts. Ask the children to consider the same events in a story from another character's point of view. You could display these accounts around the original point of view in the text and compare the versions.

Developing Literacy
Text Level Year 6
© A & C Black 2000

A personal response

Use this sheet to help you to record your thoughts about a book.

Title _____

Author _____

- Give the book a score out of ten in each category.
- Write evidence from the text in the rosettes.

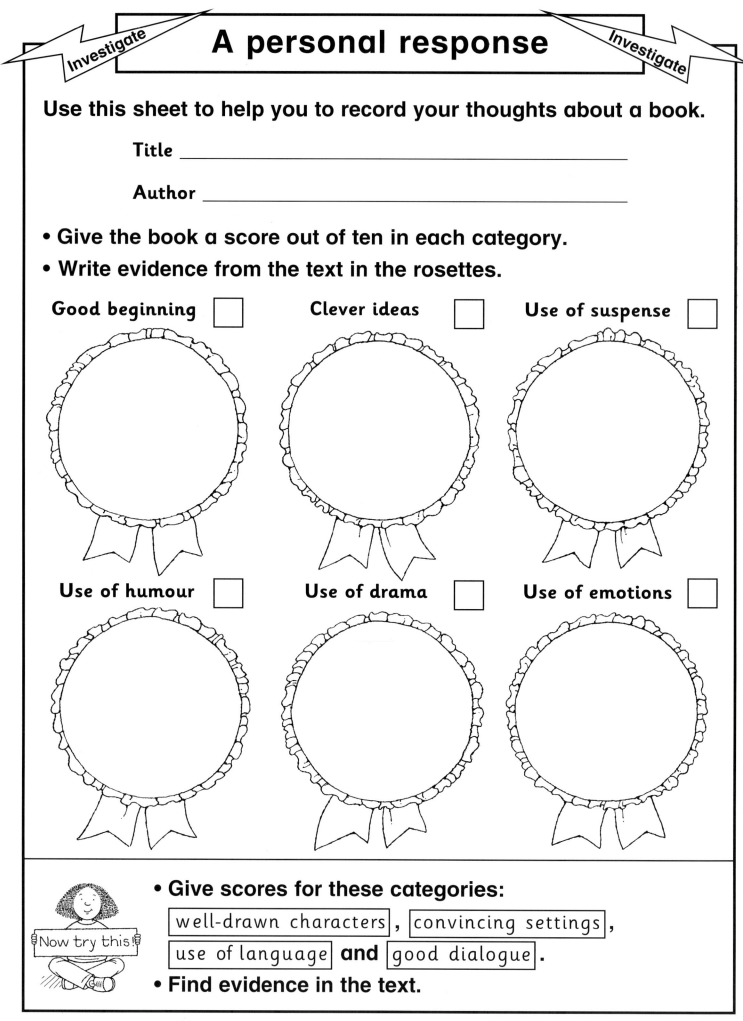

Good beginning ☐   Clever ideas ☐   Use of suspense ☐

Use of humour ☐   Use of drama ☐   Use of emotions ☐

Now try this!

- **Give scores for these categories:**
  well-drawn characters , convincing settings , use of language **and** good dialogue .
- **Find evidence in the text.**

Teachers' note It is important that the children can articulate their personal responses to a text in language specific to fiction (a metalanguage). Encourage the children to collect and list any useful phrases, for example, 'It gives me an impression of…', 'it reminds me of…' which will make the task easier in the future.

Developing Literacy
Text Level Year 6
© A & C Black 2000

Authors and their work

Use this sheet to help you to record information about an author and his or her work.

• **Find out some information about the author.**

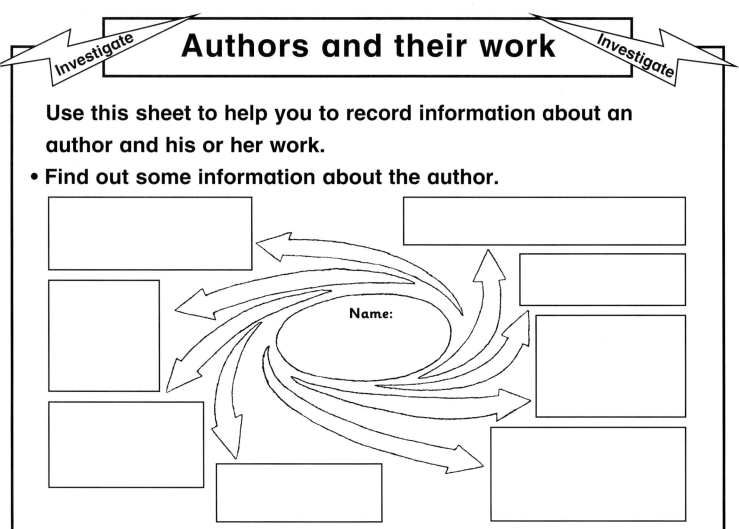

Name:

• **Put the information into a sensible order.**

1.	5.
2.	6.
3.	7.
4.	8.

• **Use your notes to write a paragraph about your author. Say what you think is special about the work of this author.**

Now try this!

• **Use a new sheet to make notes about another author. This time, concentrate on the author's** [style] **and the** [themes] **in his or her work.**

Teachers' note When dealing with 'classic' fiction, poetry and drama by long-established authors, it is useful if the children can become familiar with as much of their work as possible. You could compare what the children have discovered about the same authors and where they found the information. Has their research led to the children reading more texts by the authors?

Developing Literacy
Text Level Year 6
© A & C Black 2000

Time

- **Use this sheet to help you investigate the importance of time in a book you have read.**

Title _____

Author _____

- **What time periods are covered in the book?** ☑

Minutes ☐   Hours ☐   Days ☐   Years ☐

Evidence from the book:

_____

_____

_____

_____

- **How does time work in this book?** ☑

Does it look forward? ☐   Does it look back? ☐

Does it jump about? ☐   Does the author use flashback? ☐

Does the author play with time (as in science fiction)? ☐

Evidence from the book:

_____

_____

_____

_____

_____

_____

_____

_____

Now try this!

- **Draw a time-line listing the events in the book, with dates or times. Show how much time each section of the story takes.**

Teachers' note Use this sheet to bring out the children's understanding of a book in which the time scheme is clear. This is an important link with narrative structure. Often the handling of time in a story helps to link the chapters. In shared reading, bring out how knowing more about the way an author uses time can help the reader's understanding of what a book is about.

Developing Literacy
Text Level Year 6
© A & C Black 2000

Sentence order

The sentences in this paragraph are in the wrong order.

- Underline the [key sentence] which introduces the topic of the paragraph.

- Write the sentences in an order which makes sense.

- Give the paragraph a title.

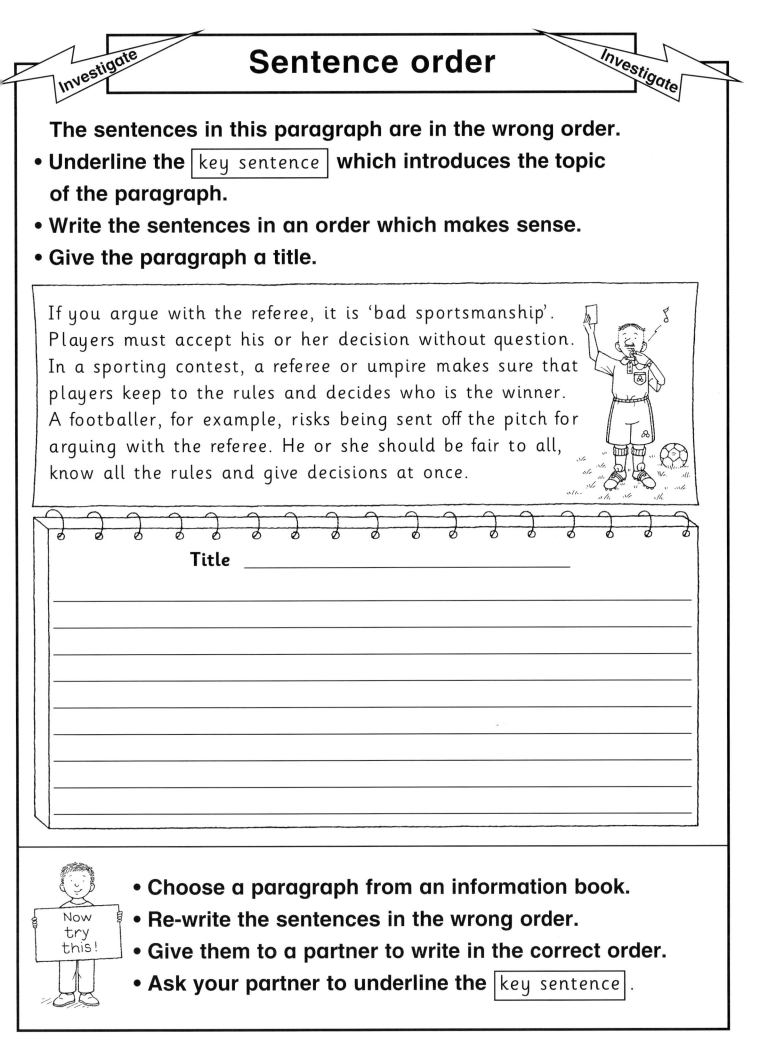

If you argue with the referee, it is 'bad sportsmanship'. Players must accept his or her decision without question. In a sporting contest, a referee or umpire makes sure that players keep to the rules and decides who is the winner. A footballer, for example, risks being sent off the pitch for arguing with the referee. He or she should be fair to all, know all the rules and give decisions at once.

Title _____

_____

_____

_____

_____

_____

_____

_____

_____

Now try this!

- **Choose a paragraph from an information book.**
- **Re-write the sentences in the wrong order.**
- **Give them to a partner to write in the correct order.**
- **Ask your partner to underline the** [key sentence].

Teachers' note This activity links with sentence-level work on complex sentences. During shared reading, you could focus on individual paragraphs in a text to discuss how they are structured. Do they follow a character's thoughts in logical order? Do they give a series of examples to prove a point? When does the subject of the writing change?

Developing Literacy
Text Level Year 6
© A & C Black 2000

Rhythm: sea-shanties

Sailors used to sing rhythmic songs called sea-shanties while they worked. The sailors raised the sails by pulling ropes in time to the rhythm of the song.

• **Read this sea-shanty.**

Blow* the man down, bullies, blow the man down,   *knock
Way, ay – blow the man down!
O, blow the man down in Liverpool Town,
Give me some time to blow the man down!

'Twas on a Black Baller* I first served my time,   *a coal ship
Way, ay – blow the man down!
And on that Black Baller I wasted my prime.
Give me some time to blow the man down!

ANONYMOUS

• **Underline the lines which are repeated. How might these have helped the sailors in their hard work?** _____

_____

• **Count the number of syllables on each line. Is there a pattern?**

_____

• **Tap out the rhythm of the lines. How many strong beats are there in each line?** _____

Now try this!

• **Complete the next verse. Follow the same rhythm and use the same repeated lines, called a** refrain.

The captain he told us the work would be hard,

_____

_____

Teachers' note Children could collect together their verses and publish them in their own 'Shanty anthology'. The best way for the children to understand the purpose of the rhythm is to give a performance of the poem. Tap out the rhythm so the children can speak the verses chorally. Include the movements which explain the rhythm.

Developing Literacy
Text Level Year 6
© A & C Black 2000

Rhyme: clerihews

These poems are called clerihews. They are named after their author, Edmund Clerihew Bentley.

- **Read the clerihews.**
- **Complete the chart to show their pattern.**

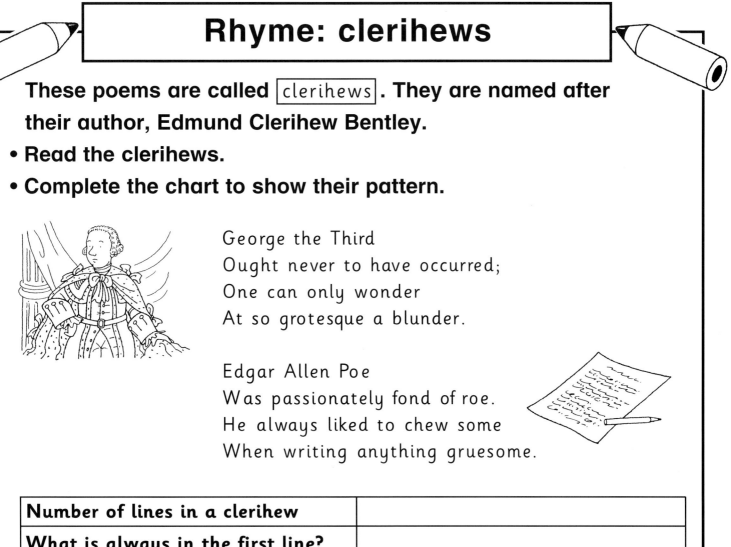

George the Third
Ought never to have occurred;
One can only wonder
At so grotesque a blunder.

Edgar Allen Poe
Was passionately fond of roe.
He always liked to chew some
When writing anything gruesome.

Number of lines in a clerihew	
What is always in the first line?	
Where are the rhymes?	
Are they serious or funny?	

- **Follow the pattern. Complete this clerihew.**

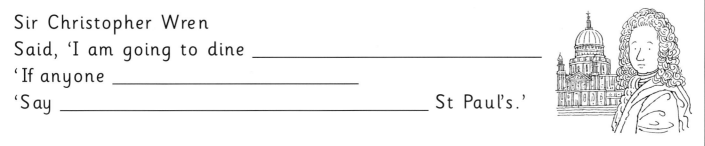

Sir Christopher Wren
Said, 'I am going to dine _____
'If anyone _____
'Say _____ St Paul's.'

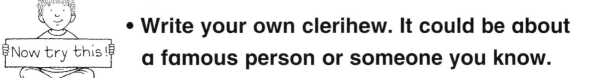

- **Write your own clerihew. It could be about a famous person or someone you know.**

Teachers' note This poetic form may seem complicated, but because the lines may be of unequal length, and the first line always concerns a person's name, it is the simple rhyme scheme – aabb – upon which the children can concentrate. The clerihews they write can be as silly as the children like! Introduce the idea of a 'rhyme scheme'.

Developing Literacy
Text Level Year 6
© A & C Black 2000

Figurative language

Figurative language uses figures of speech such as $\boxed{\text{similes}}$, $\boxed{\text{metaphors}}$ **and** $\boxed{\text{personification}}$.

- **Read the poem.**
- **Underline in** $\boxed{\text{red}}$ **an example of a** $\boxed{\text{metaphor}}$.
- **Underline in** $\boxed{\text{blue}}$ **an example of** $\boxed{\text{personification}}$.

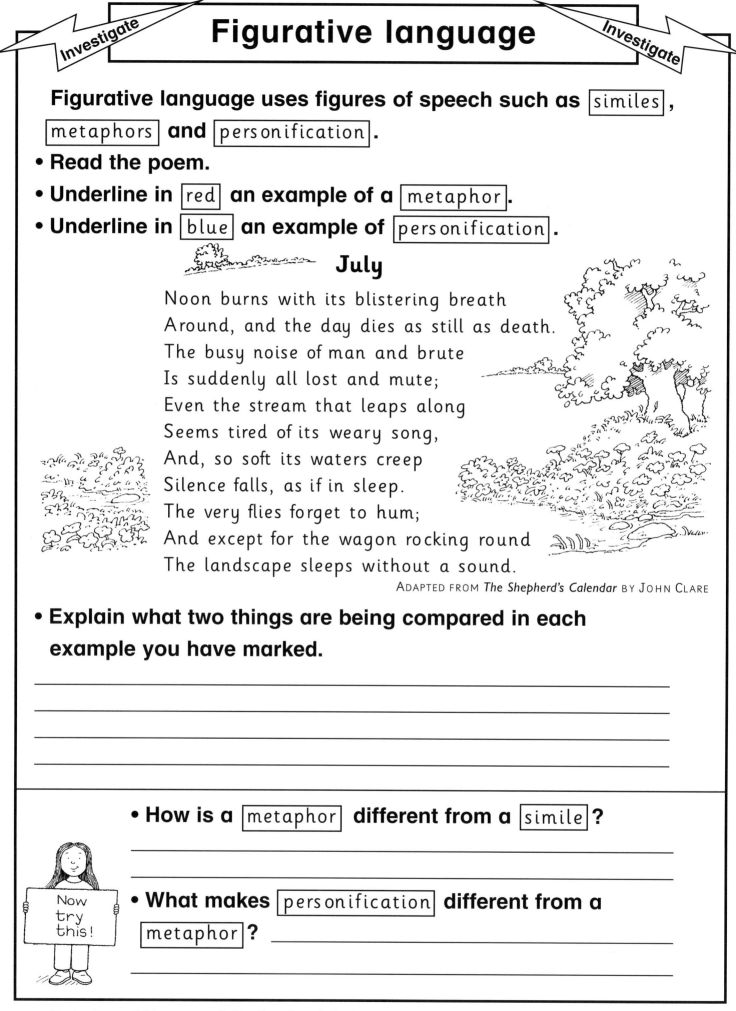

July

Noon burns with its blistering breath
Around, and the day dies as still as death.
The busy noise of man and brute
Is suddenly all lost and mute;
Even the stream that leaps along
Seems tired of its weary song,
And, so soft its waters creep
Silence falls, as if in sleep.
The very flies forget to hum;
And except for the wagon rocking round
The landscape sleeps without a sound.

ADAPTED FROM *The Shepherd's Calendar* BY JOHN CLARE

- **Explain what two things are being compared in each example you have marked.**

_____
_____
_____
_____

- **How is a** $\boxed{\text{metaphor}}$ **different from a** $\boxed{\text{simile}}$ **?**
  _____
  _____

- **What makes** $\boxed{\text{personification}}$ **different from a** $\boxed{\text{metaphor}}$ **?** _____
  _____

Now try this!

Teachers' note Children can usually identify and use similes from the words 'like' or 'as', but metaphors can be more difficult for them to grasp. During shared reading, you could point out words used metaphorically and what the comparison is. Focus on how metaphors allow multiple layers of meaning to be built up through the feelings evoked in the reader.

Developing Literacy
Text Level Year 6
© A & C Black 2000

16

Playing with language

In both these poems, the poets are playing with language.

- **Read the poems aloud. What makes them sound strange?**
- **Write out versions of the poems in standard English.**

Why have the poets used such peculiar words? Look for clues in the poems.

Try reading this poem in an American accent!

Love song to Bary Jade (Mary Jane)

The bood is beabig brighdly love,
The sdars are shidig too;
While I ab gazig dreabily
Add thigkig, love, of you;
You caddot, oh, you caddot kdow,
By darlig, how I biss you —
(Oh, whadt a fearful cold I've got —
Ck-tish-u! Ck-ck-tish-u!

ANONYMOUS

_____
_____
_____
_____
_____
_____
_____
_____
_____
_____
_____
_____
_____
_____
_____
_____

Conversation between fisherman

Hiyamac. _____
Lobuddy. _____
Binearlong? _____
Cuplours. _____
Ketchanenny? _____
Goddafew. _____
Kindarthay? _____
Bassencarp. _____
Enysizetoum? _____
Cuplapowns. _____
Hittinard? _____
Sordalite. _____
Wahchoozin? _____
Gobbawurms. _____
Fishanonaboddum? _____
_____
Rydonnaboddum. _____
_____
Igoddago. _____
Tubad. _____
Seeyaround. _____
Yeatakideezy. _____
Guluk. _____

ANONYMOUS

Now try this!

- **Write two more lines for each poem, following the pattern and playing with language in the same way.**

Teachers' note This links with sentence-level work on standard English. Concentrate on how the poets are using words for the quality of their sound and are playing with how the reader sounds the words in order for them to grasp the comic significance. Compare these poems with nonsense or humorous verse to see in which ways they are similar and different (see page 19).

Developing Literacy
Text Level Year 6
© A & C Black 2000

Ambiguity

Statements that are ambiguous have more than one meaning. Often, these make us laugh.

- Explain why these examples are funny.
- On a separate sheet, write out a version of each which is <u>not</u> ambiguous.

Ambiguous statement	Why it is funny	What the writer really means
The goalkeeper dived for the ball. He decided to head it. It came off first time.		
If your child does not like milk, try heating it slowly in boiling water.		
Pills should be kept in a cabinet. If you have children, make sure they are locked away.		
Headaches? Get your eyes tested. We can help get rid of them.		
She found a van full of sheep which had broken down.		

- Write four ambiguous statements.
- Ask a partner to explain the two possible meanings of each statement.

Teachers' note This activity links with sentence-level work, as many examples of ambiguity will be the result of misplaced pronouns. The children could make an explanatory book of these, drawing cartoons to illustrate the comic meanings when they occur.

Developing Literacy
Text Level Year 6
© A & C Black 2000

Nonsense verse

Lewis Carroll wrote a famous nonsense poem, *Jabberwocky*.

- **Read this passage, in which Humpty Dumpty tries to explain it to Alice.**

Jabberwocky

'Twas brillig, and the slithy toves
Did gyre and gimble in the wabe;
All mimsy were the borogroves,
And the mome raths outgrabe.

*

'"Brillig" means four o'clock in the
afternoon – the time when you
begin broiling things for dinner.'
'That'll do very well,' said Alice:
'and "slithy"?'
'Well, "slithy" means "lithe
and slimy". "Lithe" is the same
as "active".'

FROM *Through the Looking-glass, and what Alice found there*
BY LEWIS CARROLL

Humpty Dumpty's other explanations

"toves" = a cross between badgers, lizards
and corkscrews. They live under sun-dials.
"gyre" = to go round in a circle
"gimble" = to make holes
"wabe" = the grass around a sun-dial
"mimsy" = flimsy and miserable
"borogrove" = a thin, shabby-looking bird
with its feathers sticking out all round
"mome" = possibly short for 'from home'
(i.e. lost)
"rath" = a sort of green pig
"outgrabe" = between bellowing and
whistling, with a kind of sneeze in the middle

- **Complete the chart with your own explanations for the nonsense words in this verse.**

'Beware the Jabberwock, my son!
The jaws that bite, the claws that catch!
Beware the Jubjub bird, and shun
The frumious Bandersnatch!'

Jabberwock	
Jubjub bird	
frumious	
Bandersnatch	

- **Make a 'nonsense-word' dictionary to help others to understand *Jabberwocky*.**

Teachers' note To introduce this activity, read the whole poem to the children. Discuss how the story is recognisable, even though many of the words are new. The children could research other nonsense poems, for example, *The Owl and the Pussycat* by Edward Lear, and make collections of the unusual words, for example, what is a 'runcible spoon'?

Developing Literacy
Text Level Year 6
© **A & C Black 2000**

Moods and feelings in poetry

In dreams and nightmares, the world can look peculiar.

In this poem, the poet imagines an undersea world.

• **Think about the questions as you read the poem.**

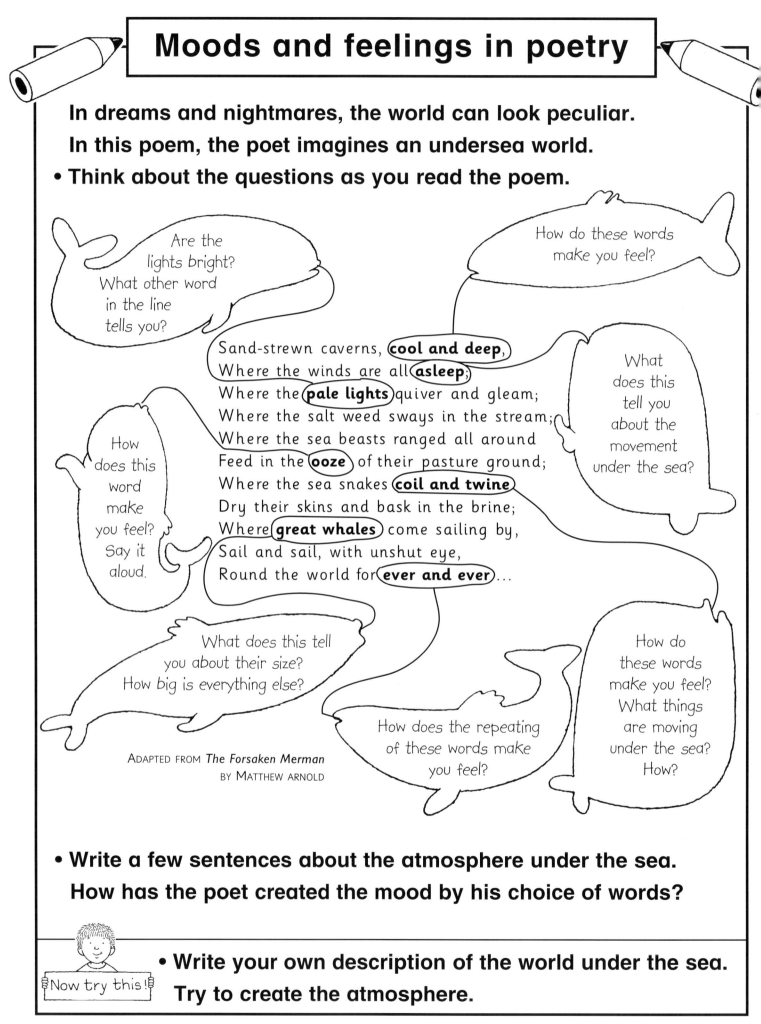

Are the lights bright? What other word in the line tells you?

How do these words make you feel?

Sand-strewn caverns, **cool and deep**,
Where the winds are all **asleep**;
Where the **pale lights** quiver and gleam;
Where the salt weed sways in the stream;
Where the sea beasts ranged all around
Feed in the **ooze** of their pasture ground;
Where the sea snakes **coil and twine**
Dry their skins and bask in the brine;
Where **great whales** come sailing by,
Sail and sail, with unshut eye,
Round the world for **ever and ever**...

What does this tell you about the movement under the sea?

How does this word make you feel? Say it aloud.

What does this tell you about their size? How big is everything else?

ADAPTED FROM *The Forsaken Merman* BY MATTHEW ARNOLD

How does the repeating of these words make you feel?

How do these words make you feel? What things are moving under the sea? How?

• **Write a few sentences about the atmosphere under the sea.**
How has the poet created the mood by his choice of words?

Now try this!

• **Write your own description of the world under the sea.**
Try to create the atmosphere.

Teachers' note The important thing is that the children should realise that there is not necessarily a 'correct' answer to these subjective questions. They should be able to discuss how the words of the poet make them feel, for example, how the poet creates an eerie, silent world, where small creatures are distorted to look sinister.

Developing Literacy
Text Level Year 6
© A & C Black 2000

Characters

• **Use this sheet to decide how important a character is in a book you are reading.**

Title _____

Name of character _____

Give evidence from the book to prove your points.

• **Give each category a score out of ten.**

The character

helps the story along	☐	_____
makes the story seem more real	☐	_____
adds to the excitement of the story	☐	_____
adds humour to the story	☐	_____
adds to the confusion	☐	_____
makes things work out in the end	☐	_____

Now try this!

• **Use your notes to write some paragraphs about how important you think the character is in the book.**

Teachers' note It is often difficult for the children to understand the function of a character in a book and hence to investigate what the writer is trying to do. Ask the children to deal with one of the ideas above at a time, always finding evidence to back their assertions. In this way they should discover that characters fulfil a specific role in a work of fiction.

Developing Literacy
Text Level Year 6
© **A & C Black 2000**

Suspense

- **Write a headline to summarise the story in each picture.**
- **Think about what might happen next in each story.**

Teachers' note During a shared writing exercise you could plan one of these stories with the children. As they come to an exciting moment, discuss what should come before it (for example, silence) – and what should come after the moment (such as, should there be more silence, a release from tension or should something dreadful happen?). Which solution do they like best?

Developing Literacy
Text Level Year 6
© A & C Black 2000

Compare and contrast

- **Cut out the headings and use them to make a poster.**
- **Under each heading, record your thoughts about the work of a writer.**

Author _____

Titles _____

_____

Place	Where are the different texts set?
Time	In which era is each text set?
Language	Is the language simple, poetic, difficult? Do the texts use different kinds of language? If so, why?
Genre	What kind of story is the writer telling? Is it historical, modern, supernatural, fantasy?
Tone	Is the work serious or funny? Does the writer use a variety of tones? If so, why?
Characters	What kind of characters does the writer usually write about? Does he or she include more heroes than villains? How do you respond to the characters? Why?
Narrator	Do the texts use the first or third person?
Conclusion	Which texts do you like best and why?

Now try this!

- **Use your notes to write about two works by the same author. Explain how they are similar or different. What do you like or dislike about them?**

Teachers' note Display the children's thoughts about the works of an author. Paste the headings and the children's responses to them around a picture of the author or the book jackets. The important outcome of this work should be that the children realise that there is not a 'correct' answer and that they need to justify their feelings with evidence from the texts.

Developing Literacy
Text Level Year 6
© A & C Black 2000

Writing about books

• **Make notes on this page to help you to structure your writing about a book you have read.**

Author _____

Title _____

Time: In which period is the book set? How does the historical detail create a special atmosphere? _____
_____
_____

Place: In which locations is the book set? What impact does the setting have on the characters and their actions? _____
_____
_____

The story-line: What is the story about? What length of time does it cover? Is the beginning exciting or slow? What is the climax of the story? How is it resolved? _____
_____
_____
_____

Characters: Which do you like best? Why? Which do you dislike the most? Why? Do the characters change through the story? How?
_____
_____
_____

Conclusions: Why do you think the author wanted to tell this story? How did you feel as you were reading it? _____
_____
_____

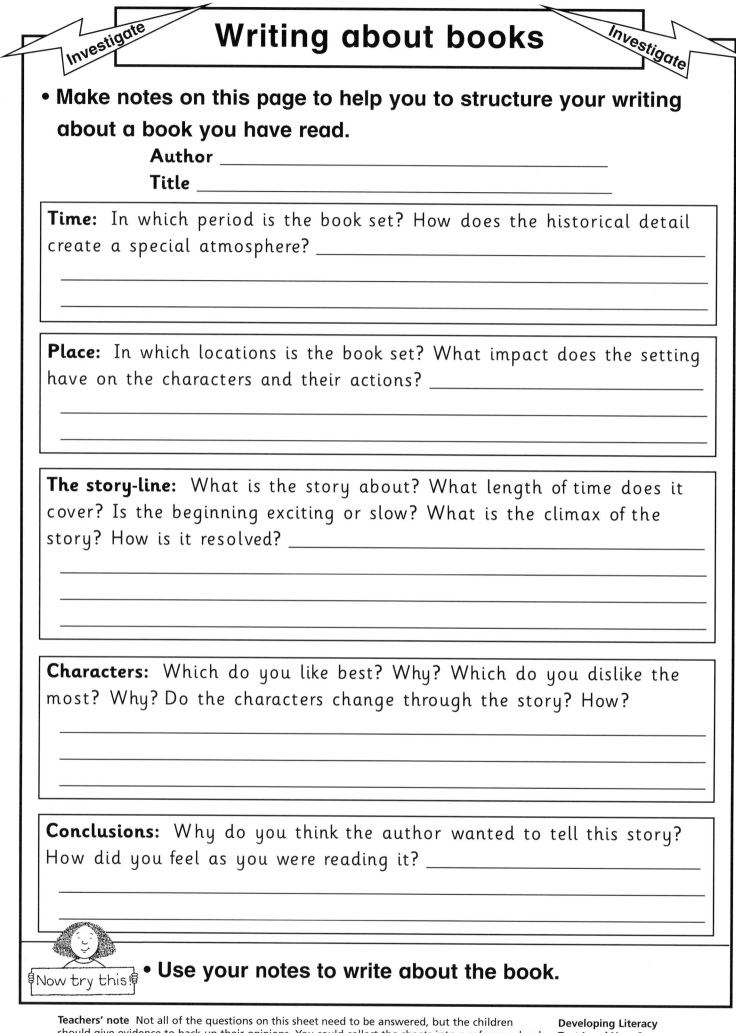

Now try this! • **Use your notes to write about the book.**

Teachers' note Not all of the questions on this sheet need to be answered, but the children should give evidence to back up their opinions. You could collect the sheets into a reference book so that they can form the basis of recommendations for wider reading. Copies of this page could be used to contrast works by different authors.

Developing Literacy
Text Level Year 6
© A & C Black 2000

A story with a moral

- **Read Aesop's story** *The fox and the goat.*

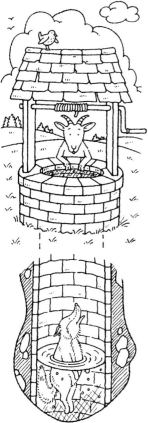

A fox had fallen down a well and was trapped. He tried to get out but it was too deep and he could not climb up the tall, straight walls. High above him, he saw a goat who had come for a drink. 'Is the water good?' asked the goat.
'I've swallowed too much of it, myself,' thought the fox, but he saw a way of getting out. 'Yes, it is wonderful,' said the silver-tongued fox. 'It is so good, I have drunk and drunk. I'm afraid I'm not feeling so well. That's why I'm resting here in the dark. You would love it.'
The goat, without more ado, leapt into the well. Just as he was reaching the water the fox jumped up and levered himself with the goat's horns until he found himself on dry land.
'Thanks for the help,' he said, as he walked off, laughing at the goat's cries for help.

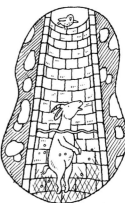

- **Complete the chart.**

What is the fox like?	
What is the goat like?	
How does the fox use the goat?	
What is the moral?	

Now try this!

- **Re-tell the story with a modern setting. Use the same types of characters, but not a fox and a goat.**

Use the same moral.

Teachers' note Model with the children how the moral can be extracted from the fable. List the character traits of the respective animals and how they could be displayed by human beings. Invite the children to put forward different scenarios set in modern times.

Developing Literacy
Text Level Year 6
© A & C Black 2000

Analyse a story

- **Use this page to analyse the structure of a story that you like.**

Title: _____

Author: _____   **Genre:** _____

Location: _____   **Period:** _____

Characters:

What kind of people are they?

_____

_____

What problems do the characters face?

_____

_____

How are these problems solved?

_____

_____

Narrative:

Who is the narrator of the story line?

_____

Are there any unusual features of the story? Describe them.

Changes from the real to the imaginary?

Dreams? Magic? Invented words?

_____

_____

_____

Theme:

What do you think the author is trying to tell you?

_____

_____

_____

Now try this!

- **Make notes on another book from a different genre.**
- **How are the characters and problems different?**

Teachers' note This sheet looks at narrative structure and particularly at how authors use characters and situations to develop plot-lines. Children should collect their sheets and compare the approaches of various genres: for example, authors of fantasy stories may find it easier to extract their characters from awkward situations by magic.

Developing Literacy
Text Level Year 6
© A & C Black 2000

Summarising

To summarise something, you write it in a shortened form.

• **Summarise on the note pad what Nimesh needs to buy.**

I need to go to the shops and buy two kilos of sugar, a kilo of onions, half a dozen free-range eggs and a small brown loaf.

Some children are organising a school disco.

'O.K. Everyone seems to agree that we should hold a summer disco in the school hall on Friday the 17th of July from 7 until 9·30 pm. Mark, you'll ask tomorrow, but if that date is booked we'll go for Monday the 20th. We need to get the tickets made by the 1st of July. Maggie has agreed to ask her brother if he will be a DJ – his discos are always really popular. But we only have £20. Kim will do the poster again – thanks, Kim. Now the poster needs to warn people that the price this year has gone up to £2, but it is in a good cause – for the refugees. Now, food – Mike, will you ask your mum again? Her pizzas are brilliant. Great. Thanks.

POSTCARD

Place: school hall

Now try this!

• **Compare your summary with a partner's.**

Teachers' note Model with the children how to extract the relevant information, such as by underlining, in order to write in their own words.

Developing Literacy
Text Level Year 6
© A & C Black 2000

27

Write a story as a playscript

• **Read the extract from an Indian myth about Krishna.**

Krishna and the Snake King

Kaliya was the king of the snakes. He had five heads which breathed fire and he lived under the whirlpools of the Yamuna River. He would come to the surface, cause terror, steal the cows and take them back to his court under the water.

One day the cowherds came to Krishna, who was only twelve, to ask for his help. Krishna took his friends to the river. Suddenly the snake rose up, grabbed the mortals and dragged them below. Krishna waited until Kaliya emerged again, jumped on his five heads and crushed two under his arms. The snake dragged him down. Krishna continued to dance on Kaliya's remaining three heads. At last Kaliya was left with just one head, and as he reached his underwater court, Krishna broke it off.

Krishna revived his dead friends with the magic of the gods and brought them back to the surface so that they could tend their cows once more.

• **On a separate sheet, write the extract as a playscript. Follow the dramatic conventions.**

Dramatic conventions
- Divided into acts and scenes.
- Paragraph to set the scene.
- Characters' names on the left.
- No speech marks. New line for what each character says.
- Stage directions for actions in italics.
- Prompts to actors in italics and in brackets.

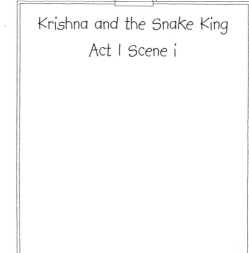

Krishna and the Snake King
Act I Scene i

Now try this!

• **Ask a partner to check your script against the list of dramatic conventions.**

Teachers' note Remind the children about the functions of the dramatic conventions, for example, the prompts for actors so that the actors can convey to the audience what feelings lie behind the words. What kind of stage directions do the children think would improve the dramatic performance potential?

Developing Literacy
Text Level Year 6
© A & C Black 2000

'Strong' verbs

- **Read this description of a river.**
- **Underline the verbs.**
- **Circle the ending they have in common.**

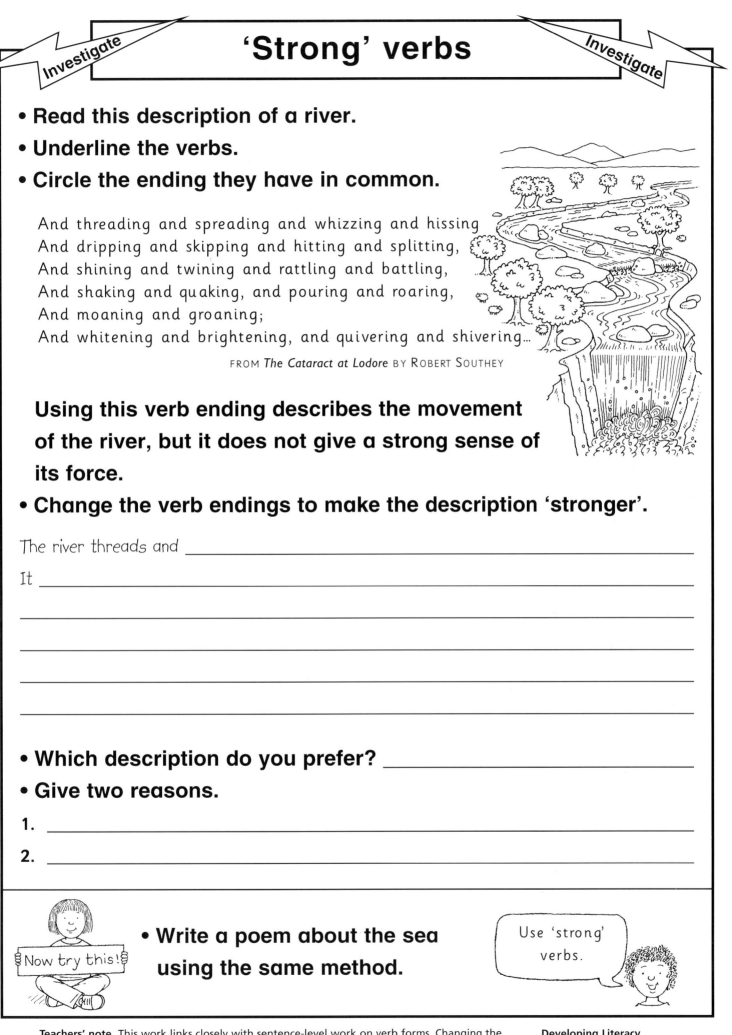

And threading and spreading and whizzing and hissing
And dripping and skipping and hitting and splitting,
And shining and twining and rattling and battling,
And shaking and quaking, and pouring and roaring,
And moaning and groaning;
And whitening and brightening, and quivering and shivering...

FROM *The Cataract at Lodore* BY ROBERT SOUTHEY

Using this verb ending describes the movement of the river, but it does not give a strong sense of its force.

- **Change the verb endings to make the description 'stronger'.**

The river threads and _____

It _____

_____

_____

_____

_____

- **Which description do you prefer?** _____
- **Give two reasons.**

1. _____

2. _____

Now try this!

- **Write a poem about the sea using the same method.**

Use 'strong' verbs.

Teachers' note This work links closely with sentence-level work on verb forms. Changing the verbs from the present continuous makes the verbs create an impression of forceful action and not merely act as description. Show how the poet has chosen the form of the verb to suggest the movement of the fast-flowing water through the rhythm.

Developing Literacy
Text Level Year 6
© A & C Black 2000

Personification

| Personification | **is a form of** | metaphor | **. It gives something human features or emotions.**

- **Read the poem. Think about the answers to the questions.**

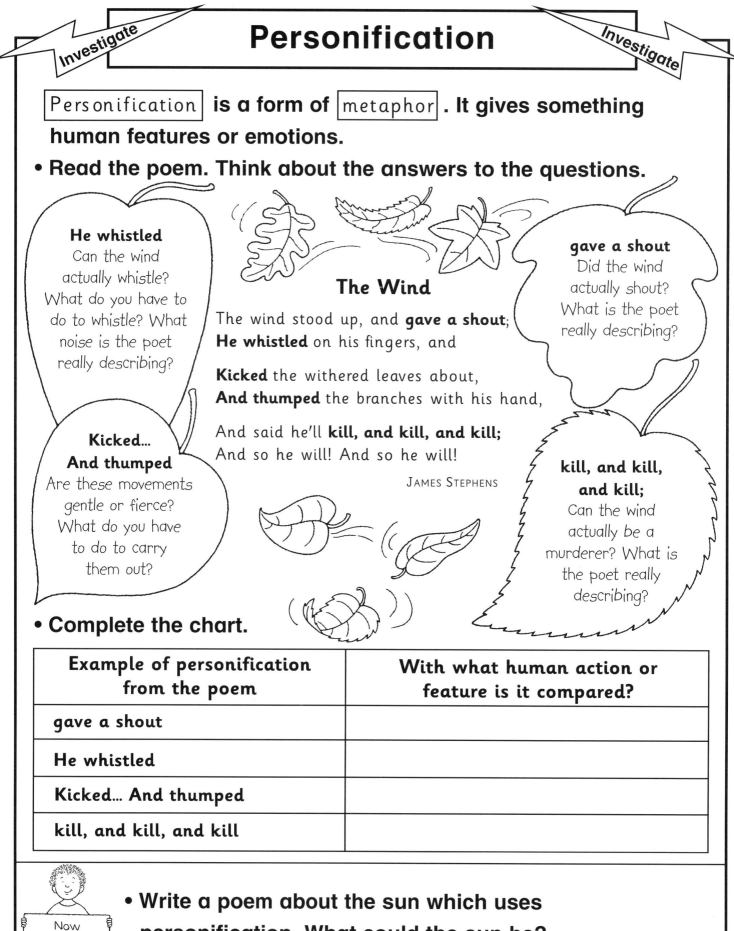

He whistled
Can the wind actually whistle? What do you have to do to whistle? What noise is the poet really describing?

Kicked...
And thumped
Are these movements gentle or fierce? What do you have to do to carry them out?

The Wind

The wind stood up, and **gave a shout**;
He whistled on his fingers, and

Kicked the withered leaves about,
And thumped the branches with his hand,

And said he'll **kill, and kill, and kill;**
And so he will! And so he will!

JAMES STEPHENS

gave a shout
Did the wind actually shout? What is the poet really describing?

kill, and kill, and kill;
Can the wind actually be a murderer? What is the poet really describing?

- **Complete the chart.**

Example of personification from the poem	With what human action or feature is it compared?
gave a shout	
He whistled	
Kicked... And thumped	
kill, and kill, and kill	

Now try this!

- **Write a poem about the sun which uses personification. What could the sun be? What human features could the sun have?**

Teachers' note Discuss with the children the human features of the wind as described in the poem and what they represent. You could make a list of other human characteristics it could have, such as its breath, and note these for later guided writing activities.

Developing Literacy
Text Level Year 6
© A & C Black 2000

Flashbacks

A story needs a beginning, middle and end. Do they always have to come in that order?

• **Cut out the cards. Think about how you could tell the story in different ways, by changing the order of the cards.**

It couldn't have been
a finer day for a bike ride...

'Look at the sky,' whispered
John, 'I'd better hurry or...'

He raced and he raced
against the storm but suddenly...

'What on Earth happened to you?'
John's father gasped...

Now try this!

• **Which is the best version of the story? Does it start at the beginning, in the middle or at the end?**
• **Write the version you think is best.**

Teachers' note During shared reading, model with the children the ways in which stories use the flashback technique to great effect. They often start at the moment of action and then work back through the events to explain what happened. They could even move forward in time to explain what happens next. The children could draw time-lines to illustrate these movements.

Developing Literacy
Text Level Year 6
© A & C Black 2000

Parody

- **When you** parody **a poem, you use the poem's style and pattern to make fun of the poem.**
- **Read these parodies.**

Humpty Dumpty sat on a wall;
Humpty Dumpty had a great fall.
All the king's horses suddenly knew
They could do nothing – they'd
forgotten the glue!

Mary had a little lamb,
It was brainless we all knew,
It tried to cross the road with her,
And now it's in a stew!

- **Write the original poems.**

Humpty Dumpty

Mary had

- **Underline the parts of the original that have been changed.**
- **Think about how the originals have been made fun of.**

- **Complete this parody in your own words.**

Original
Twinkle, twinkle, little star,
How I wonder what you are!
Up above the world so high,
Like a diamond in the sky.

Parody
Twinkle, twinkle, little _____
How I wonder _____
Up above the _____
Like a _____ in the _____

Now try this!

- **Write your own parodies of two more nursery rhymes. Work out the patterns of the nursery rhymes first.**

Teachers' note Advertisements provide good examples of parodies and often the children will know these by heart. You could use these as models to bring out how the humour was created by awareness and manipulation of the style and form of the original.

**Developing Literacy
Text Level Year 6
© A & C Black 2000**

Shop signs

Writers often play with the meanings and sounds of words.

- **Explain how these shop signs play with language.**

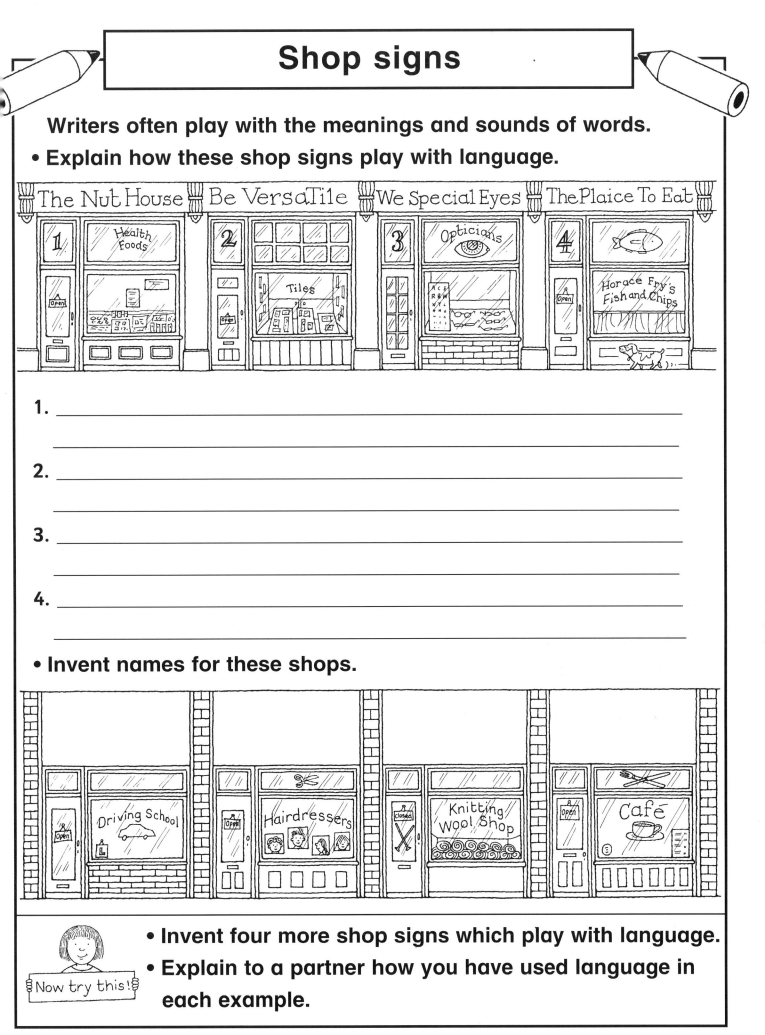

1. _____

_____

2. _____

_____

3. _____

_____

4. _____

_____

- **Invent names for these shops.**

- **Invent four more shop signs which play with language.**
- **Explain to a partner how you have used language in each example.**

Teachers' note Model the idea by collecting jokes and puns which play with words. This links with word-level work on homophones, for example, plaice/place.

Developing Literacy
Text Level Year 6
© A & C Black 2000

How to annotate a passage

- **Read the passage.**
- **Underline in** [red] **any words which tell you about the location.**
- **Underline in** [blue] **any words which tell you how Sheena felt.**

The moon had just disappeared behind the clouds. Among the forest trees the night was pitch-black. Sheena moved carefully and silently, crawling through the grass, feeling the cold ground with her hands as she went. She knew she was near the meeting place. Just then, a twig snapped under her foot. It cracked like a gunshot. She stopped, shaking with terror. She was sure that the guards, awake and carrying rifles, had heard her. She waited, hardly daring to breathe. Below her, Sheena could just glimpse the inky black water of Lake Geneva. She wished she had never offered to take the message. Far away to her left, an owl hooted and a fox barked; then everything was silent again. She started to creep forward, more carefully than ever. It seemed hours before she came to the path. 'Stop!' a voice called in the darkness.

- **(Circle) the words and phrases which help to create a mysterious atmosphere.**
- **[Box] the words and phrases which help to create suspense.**
- **Find evidence in the text to support these aspects of Sheena's character:**

brave	
clever	
foolish	

- **Copy out a short passage from a book.**
- **Make up some questions to ask a partner.**
- **Ask him or her to annotate the text to show the answers.**

Now try this

Teachers' note During shared-text work, you could ask the children to identify features of text and character and to point them out by underlining them on an acetate overlay. Then ask them to justify their choice, using their own words.

Developing Literacy
Text Level Year 6
© A & C Black 2000

A reading journal

Name: | **Date:**

Title:

Author: | **Fiction or non-fiction:**

Other books I have read by this author

What made me read this book

What the book is about

Location of the book

Characters in the book

What I thought of the book

Now try this!

- **Use your notes to write an account of the book.**
- **Find out about the author and other books he or she has written.**

Teachers' note Ask the children to complete this sheet regularly and to collect their findings. At the end of every term, they can reconsider their reading habits and think about whether their opinions have changed. You could make a class collection of sheets on specific authors or on non-fiction text-types of different curriculum areas.

Developing Literacy
Text Level Year 6
© A & C Black 2000

'Blurb'

- **Choose a book you know well.**
- **How would you write a back-cover 'blurb' for a new edition?**
- **Think about:**

  your aim – what is the purpose of a back-cover 'blurb'?

  your audience – who will be reading your 'blurb'?

- **You could include:**

questions to interest people

How? What? When? Where? Why? Who?

quotations from the first chapter

Don't give too much away!

quotations from a reviewer

'A brilliant read.'

information about the author

other useful information

Are there any other books in the series?

- **Now write your 'blurb'.**

Title _____

- **Make a collection of back-cover 'blurbs'.**
- **Analyse them using the information on this page.**
  Do they contain any other features?

Now try this!

Teachers' note You could look at various books and analyse the content and the style of the 'blurbs'. The children need to understand the purpose of the writing and how persuasive it needs to be using evidence all the time. The children could design new covers for the titles, based on the back-cover copy only.

Developing Literacy
Text Level Year 6
© A & C Black 2000

A book review

Title _____

Author _____

This book was about	My favourite part of the story was
My favourite character was because	
	because
	The part I liked least was because
The character I most disliked was because	
	I recommend/do not recommend this book because

• **Write a different kind of book review (for example, you could design a certificate to be awarded to the author). Give your reasons for your opinions.**

Teachers' note This is an opportunity for the children to give their real views about books which they have read. Remind them that there is no 'correct' answer and that they might dislike a book. Emphasise that they should always be able to back up their ideas with evidence.

Developing Literacy
Text Level Year 6
© A & C Black 2000

Write a riddle

Riddles are puzzles. They describe familiar things as though they are something else.

- **Read these riddles. Complete the chart.**

Riddle	Clues	Answer
A skin have I, More eyes than one. I can be nice when I am done.		
You use it between your head and toes, The more it works, the thinner it grows.		
Four fingers and a thumb Yet flesh and bone have I none.		

- **Complete this riddle about a chair.**

I have four legs,

Follow these 'handy hints for riddlers'.

- Your riddle does not need a title.
- Imagine you are the thing you are describing.
- Use accurate detail, but make it sound strange.
- Only describe one thing.
- Don't say too much. Keep it short!

Now try this!

- **Write two more riddles about pieces of furniture.**

Teachers' note As an introduction to the activity, you could read the part of *The Hobbit* by JRR Tolkien in which Gollum and Bilbo have a riddle competition. See if the children can guess the answers to the riddles. Model how to write a riddle with the children following the rules.

Developing Literacy
Text Level Year 6
© A & C Black 2000

Biographies

- **A** biography **is an account of someone else's life.**
- **Read the extracts. Tick the ones that are from biographies.**

1. Martin Luther King was one of the most important men of American history in the twentieth century. When he was killed in 1968, the world mourned.

☐

2. I never knew what it was like to have fun until my father moved us all to that island. We had been living in the middle of London for all my life and now we were surrounded by palm trees.

☐

3. When Tutankhamun was buried, we know there must have been a great ceremony. In the tomb, even in 1922, were the remains of the feast. He was a 'boy king' but we now know he was important in returning to Egypt the worship of the ancient gods.

☐

4. 'Martin Luther King? Yes, I knew him. In my view he is one of the most important men of American history in the twentieth century. When he was killed in 1968, I was devastated.'

☐

- **Which pronouns are used in a biography?** _____
- **In which tense are biographies written?** _____
- **Complete the chart.**

Extract	Biography or not?	How I know
1.		
2.		
3.		
4.		

Now try this!

- **Find an example of a biography.**
- **Read the first page and note down some of the features you notice, for example, verb tenses.**

Teachers' note Model with the children characteristics of biography – especially the use of the third person and (usually) the past tense. Discuss with the children any biographies they have read. Use this page with page 40 and compare the features of biography with those of autobiography.

Developing Literacy
Text Level Year 6
© A & C Black 2000

Autobiographies

An autobiography is an account of your own life.

- **Read the extracts. Tick the ones that are from autobiographies.**

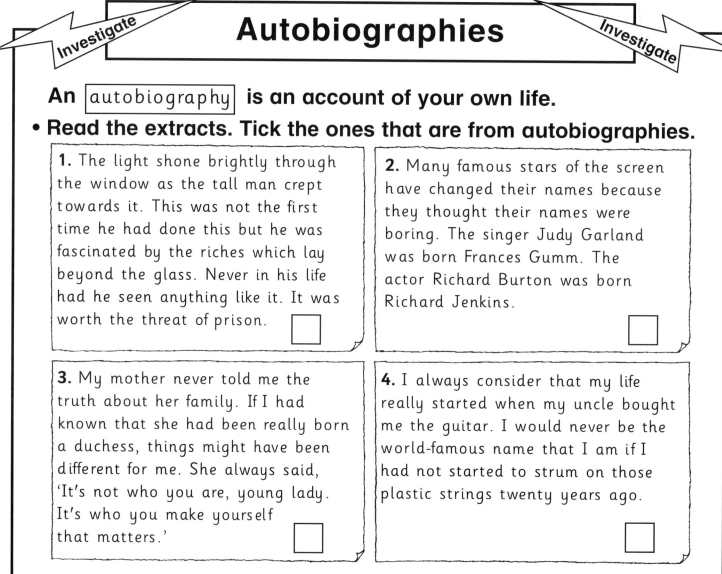

1. The light shone brightly through the window as the tall man crept towards it. This was not the first time he had done this but he was fascinated by the riches which lay beyond the glass. Never in his life had he seen anything like it. It was worth the threat of prison. ☐

2. Many famous stars of the screen have changed their names because they thought their names were boring. The singer Judy Garland was born Frances Gumm. The actor Richard Burton was born Richard Jenkins. ☐

3. My mother never told me the truth about her family. If I had known that she had been really born a duchess, things might have been different for me. She always said, 'It's not who you are, young lady. It's who you make yourself that matters.' ☐

4. I always consider that my life really started when my uncle bought me the guitar. I would never be the world-famous name that I am if I had not started to strum on those plastic strings twenty years ago. ☐

- **Which pronouns are used in an autobiography?** _____
- **In which tense are autobiographies written?** _____

Extract	Autobiography or not?	How I know
1.		
2.		
3.		
4.		

Now try this!

- **Find an example of an autobiography.**
- **Read the first page and write down some of the features you notice, such as verb tenses.**

Teachers' note Model with the children the characteristics of autobiography – especially the use of the first person. Discuss with children any autobiographies they have read, (such as *Boy* by Roald Dahl). Use this page with page 39 and compare the features of autobiography with those of biography.

**Developing Literacy
Text Level Year 6
© A & C Black 2000**

Reports

- ## Read the report on dinosaurs.

Dinosaurs

We tend to think of dinosaurs as being the man-eaters of 'Jurassic Park', but experts tells us that many, including brachiosaurus, were vegetarians. They ate up to a ton of vegetation a day, chewing it slowly and swallowing stones to help them grind up the materials in their stomachs. Dinosaurs were reptiles – they laid eggs in nests. Scientists know this because fossils of the eggs have been found. We now think of reptiles such as crocodiles but dinosaurs walked upright, so they were able to move quickly. One surprising thing which we do not know is what their skins were like, for example, what colour dinosaurs were. While their fossilised bones remain, their skins were the first thing to decompose. They could have been any colour; scientists only think they were dull green for camouflage purposes. Imagine a pink dinosaur with yellow spots!

- ## Find an example of each of these features in the report.

1. Reports start with the general.

_____

2. Then they describe something in particular.

_____

3. They make general statements, for example, 'People say that…'

_____

4. Reports are not written in chronological order.

_____

5. Reports describe or make something clearer.

_____

6. They include use of the present tense.

_____

Now try this!

- ## Label the same features in another report.

Teachers' note To introduce the activity you could model with the children the features of a report. Discuss the reasons for these features in the various kinds of reports. The children could make a chart of the different features.

Developing Literacy
Text Level Year 6
© A & C Black 2000

Leaflets

- **Leaflets tell us important things in a simple and attractive way.**
- **Read the leaflet. Write what its purpose could be.**

KEEP YOUR CHILD SAFE
FROM THE SUN ON HOLIDAY.

Better to be safe than sorry!

Wherever you go on holiday, a child is at risk from sunshine. If you are going to a sunny climate, then you need to be extra careful.

- Keep children out of the sun between 11 a.m. and 3 p.m.
- Use a high-factor sun cream.
- Make sure they wear hats and long-sleeved, loose clothes.
- If your child is under six months old, keep him or her out of direct sun altogether.

Too much exposure to the sun can lead to problems in later life. The Sun Advisory Bureau (SAB) is here to help, 24 hours a day.

Phone us on 0999000 11122
E-mail: sab@sab.co.org
Find us at
3 Sunny Street, London.

Danger – your children need protection from the sun

- **Draw lines to show where the features of a leaflet can be found in the text.**

| Main heading or headline |
| Sub-heading or clever catchphrase |
| Main message |
| Bullet points |
| Pictures and maps |
| Details to clarify the information |
| Contact information |
| Conclusion |

- **Find a leaflet which tries to persuade you to buy something.**
- **Work with a partner. See if it contains the same features as the leaflet on this page.**

Now try this!

Teachers' note Look at a variety of leaflets – 'public information' leaflets and ones which are more commercial. Model with the children the kinds of features they have. Discuss why certain kinds of brochures focus on these features. You could make a wall display labelling the features of the leaflets.

Developing Literacy
Text Level Year 6
© A & C Black 2000

Journalism

- **Cut out the sections of the newspaper article and the labels.**
- **Arrange the sections in the correct order.**
- **Put the labels next to the correct sections.**

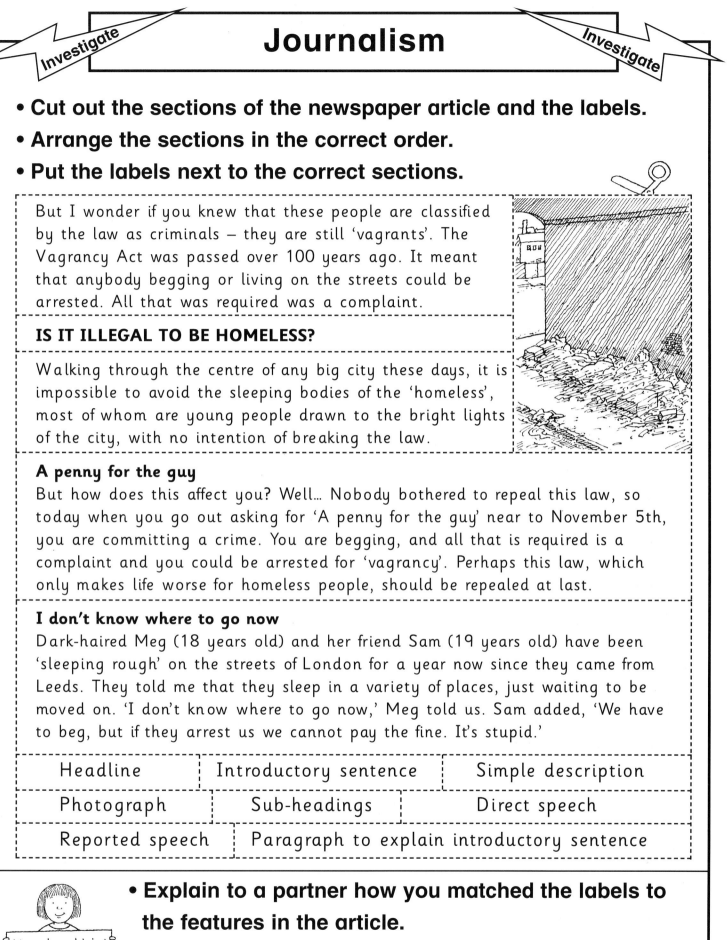

But I wonder if you knew that these people are classified by the law as criminals – they are still 'vagrants'. The Vagrancy Act was passed over 100 years ago. It meant that anybody begging or living on the streets could be arrested. All that was required was a complaint.

IS IT ILLEGAL TO BE HOMELESS?

Walking through the centre of any big city these days, it is impossible to avoid the sleeping bodies of the 'homeless', most of whom are young people drawn to the bright lights of the city, with no intention of breaking the law.

A penny for the guy
But how does this affect you? Well… Nobody bothered to repeal this law, so today when you go out asking for 'A penny for the guy' near to November 5th, you are committing a crime. You are begging, and all that is required is a complaint and you could be arrested for 'vagrancy'. Perhaps this law, which only makes life worse for homeless people, should be repealed at last.

I don't know where to go now
Dark-haired Meg (18 years old) and her friend Sam (19 years old) have been 'sleeping rough' on the streets of London for a year now since they came from Leeds. They told me that they sleep in a variety of places, just waiting to be moved on. 'I don't know where to go now,' Meg told us. Sam added, 'We have to beg, but if they arrest us we cannot pay the fine. It's stupid.'

Headline	Introductory sentence	Simple description
Photograph	Sub-headings	Direct speech
Reported speech	Paragraph to explain introductory sentence	

Now try this!

- **Explain to a partner how you matched the labels to the features in the article.**
- **Find an article from a newspaper. See if it contains the same features as the article on this page.**

Teachers' note This sheet also serves to discuss paragraphing – see pages 13 and 63 – as the structure of this narrative is especially important. The children collect different examples of newspaper articles and make a large wall display labelling the features of pieces of journalism.

**Developing Literacy
Text Level Year 6
© A & C Black 2000**

Non-chronological reports

Non-chronological reports **are not organised in a time sequence.**
- **Read the report about Luxor in Egypt.**
- **Draw lines to show where the features of a non-chronological report can be found in the text.**

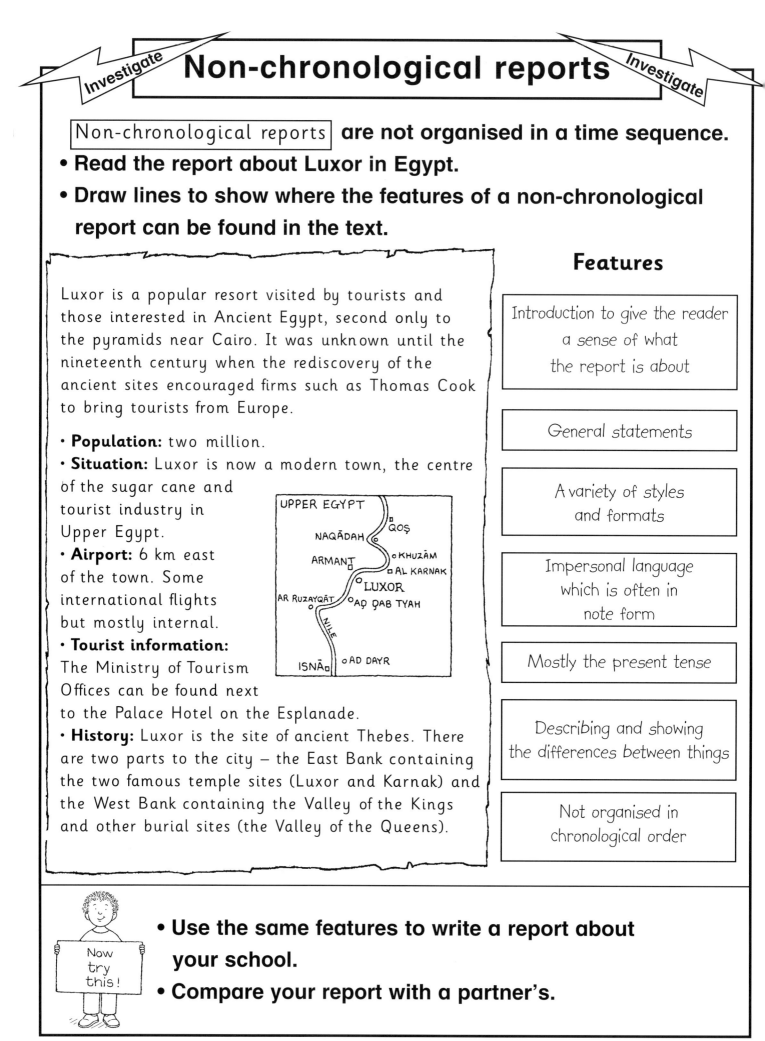

Luxor is a popular resort visited by tourists and those interested in Ancient Egypt, second only to the pyramids near Cairo. It was unknown until the nineteenth century when the rediscovery of the ancient sites encouraged firms such as Thomas Cook to bring tourists from Europe.

- **Population:** two million.
- **Situation:** Luxor is now a modern town, the centre of the sugar cane and tourist industry in Upper Egypt.
- **Airport:** 6 km east of the town. Some international flights but mostly internal.
- **Tourist information:** The Ministry of Tourism Offices can be found next to the Palace Hotel on the Esplanade.
- **History:** Luxor is the site of ancient Thebes. There are two parts to the city – the East Bank containing the two famous temple sites (Luxor and Karnak) and the West Bank containing the Valley of the Kings and other burial sites (the Valley of the Queens).

UPPER EGYPT
QOŞ
NAQĀDAH
ARMANT
KHUZĀM
AL KARNAK
LUXOR
AR RUZAYQĀT
AD DAB TYAH
NILE
ISNĀ
AD DAYR

Features

Introduction to give the reader a sense of what the report is about

General statements

A variety of styles and formats

Impersonal language which is often in note form

Mostly the present tense

Describing and showing the differences between things

Not organised in chronological order

Now try this!

- **Use the same features to write a report about your school.**
- **Compare your report with a partner's.**

Teachers' note You could look at a variety of non-chronological reports from history and geography. Point out to the children the kinds of features they have. Discuss why writing for some curriculum areas has more of these features.

Developing Literacy
Text Level Year 6
© A & C Black 2000

Explanations

- **Use this sheet to help you to identify the features of an explanation.**

Cat flu (Feline Influenza)

The symptoms of cat flu are runny eyes and nose, sneezing, producing a lot of saliva and, later, blockage of the lungs. Your cat should be kept quiet and warm until the vet arrives.

Because cats can die of this disease, rapid treatment and careful nursing are essential.

It is important to know that cats of all ages can get cat flu but it is most likely to occur in catteries or pet shops where animals are crowded together.

So it is best not to buy cats from shops. Once your cat has had flu it will carry the virus with it for the rest of its life.

However, you can have your cat injected against 'feline influenza' which will stop all this worry.

- **What should the first statement in an explanation be about?**

_____

- **In what order should an explanation be written?** _____

_____

- **Which words at the beginning of each paragraph help you to follow the order of the explanation?** _____

_____

- **In which tense is this explanation mostly written?** _____

_____

Now try this!

- **Find an example of another kind of explanation. See if it contains the same features.**

Teachers' note Look at a variety of explanations and model with the children the kinds of features they have. Discuss when explanatory texts become instructional and how the use of verbs (the imperative) tells you this.

Developing Literacy
Text Level Year 6
© A & C Black 2000

Construct an argument

- On each step, write a point for or against the argument.

The points you make need to be in a sequence.

Subject of the argument:

What evidence can you find to back the points you make? Your points need persuasive examples.

How will you answer people who object to what you say?

What do people usually say or think about this subject? How can you make use of this?

What is the first point you want to make?

What is the second point you want to make?

5. Conclusion:

4.

3.

2.

1.

- Use the notes from your steps. Write the argument in paragraphs.
- Give it to a partner to see if it can be made clearer and more persuasive.

Now try this!

Teachers' note This sheet, which could be photocopied to A3 size, should enable children to structure their writing on any argumentative text. You could discuss how best to use connectives to join the paragraphs in a logical and stylish way. Look at rhetorical devices, for example: questions, or making use of people's preconceived ideas.

Developing Literacy
Text Level Year 6
© A & C Black 2000

A balanced argument

This is the Chinese symbol of balance.

- **Use it to help you to write both sides of an argument.**

Give examples and evidence to back up your views.

Subject of argument _____

Your arguments for...   Your arguments against...

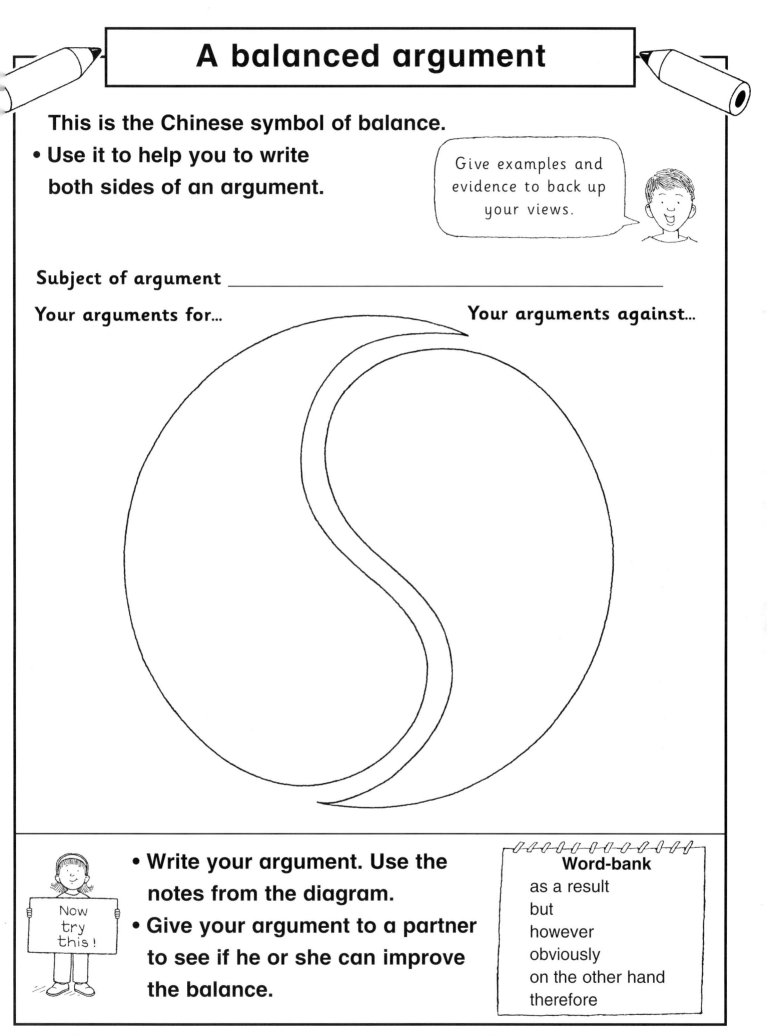

- **Write your argument. Use the notes from the diagram.**
- **Give your argument to a partner to see if he or she can improve the balance.**

Now try this!

Word-bank
as a result
but
however
obviously
on the other hand
therefore

Teachers' note This links with page 46. Arguments need to be clear, structured and well balanced to achieve their purpose. Discuss the use of 'argument words'. Look at rhetorical devices, such as questions or making use of people's preconceived ideas.

Developing Literacy
Text Level Year 6
© A & C Black 2000

Official language

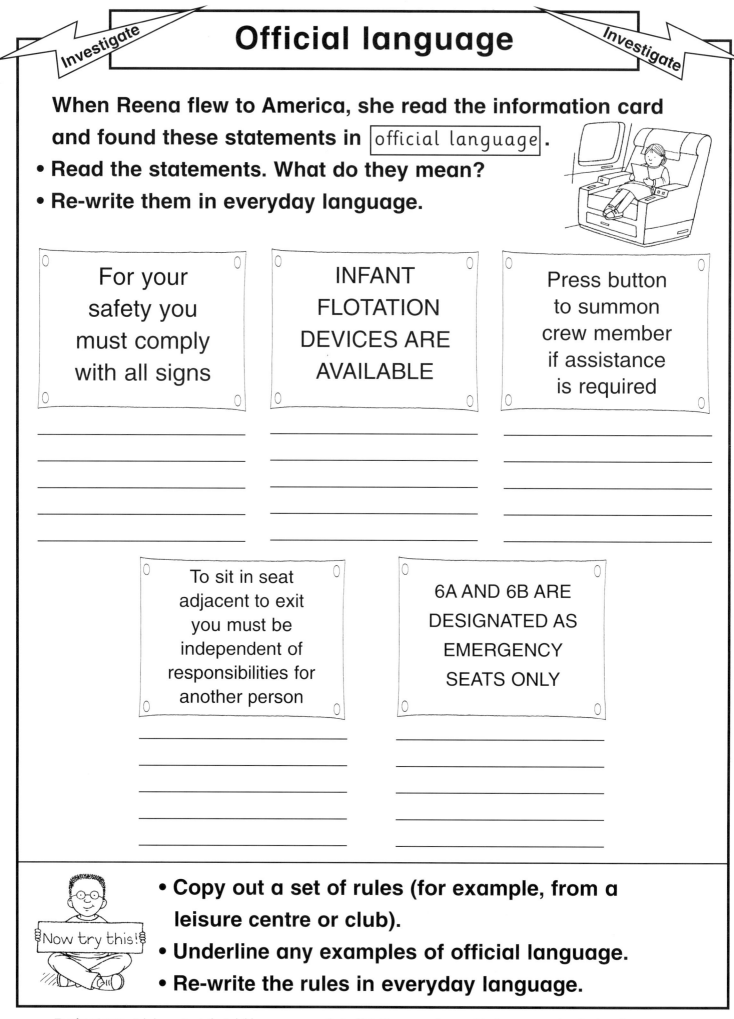

When Reena flew to America, she read the information card and found these statements in official language .

- Read the statements. What do they mean?
- Re-write them in everyday language.

For your safety you must comply with all signs

INFANT FLOTATION DEVICES ARE AVAILABLE

Press button to summon crew member if assistance is required

To sit in seat adjacent to exit you must be independent of responsibilities for another person

6A AND 6B ARE DESIGNATED AS EMERGENCY SEATS ONLY

Now try this!

- Copy out a set of rules (for example, from a leisure centre or club).
- Underline any examples of official language.
- Re-write the rules in everyday language.

Teachers' note It is important that children are aware that official language is meant to be a common language, with words and phrases acceptable to all. You could ask the children to find examples of official language, from application forms, public service signs and so on.

Developing Literacy
Text Level Year 6
© A & C Black 2000

Impersonal language

Some texts (such as scientific explanations) use
impersonal language . They feature accurate and
technical words.

• **Look at the diagrams. Think about where they might be found.**

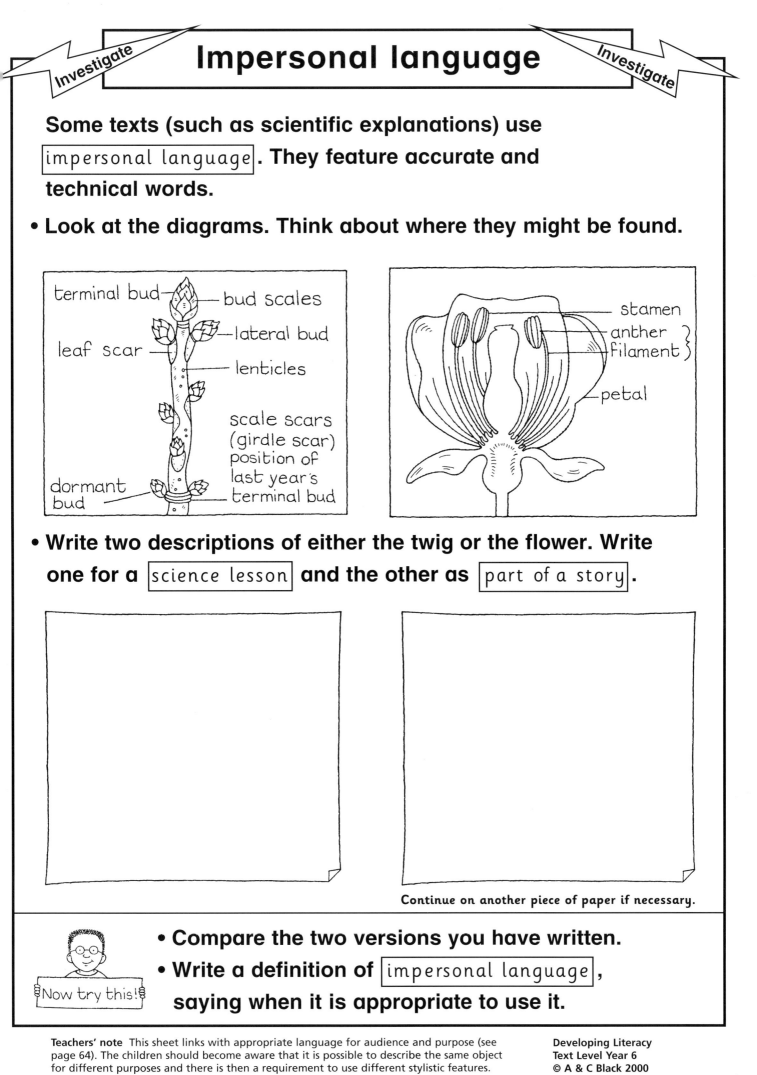

terminal bud — bud scales

— lateral bud

leaf scar — lenticles

scale scars
(girdle scar)
position of
last year's
terminal bud

dormant
bud

stamen
anther }
filament }

petal

• **Write two descriptions of either the twig or the flower. Write
one for a** science lesson **and the other as** part of a story **.**

Continue on another piece of paper if necessary.

Now try this!

• **Compare the two versions you have written.**
• **Write a definition of** impersonal language **,
saying when it is appropriate to use it.**

Teachers' note This sheet links with appropriate language for audience and purpose (see
page 64). The children should become aware that it is possible to describe the same object
for different purposes and there is then a requirement to use different stylistic features.

**Developing Literacy
Text Level Year 6
© A & C Black 2000**

Use a dictionary.

• **Read the passage. Label the diagram with information from it.**

In ancient times, people thought that the Earth was a flat disc. Over the disc was the Dome of the Heavens. Above this dome was a watery layer, 'the waters over the Earth'. This was where the rain came from — through trap-doors.

Around the flat Earth were the seas, like a moat around a castle. High mountains kept in this water and supported the heavens.

Below the Earth was the dark area of Hades, where the spirits of the dead lived. Under this were the 'waters under the Earth'.

Now try this!

• **Write a description of an object in science.**

• **Ask a partner to draw a labelled diagram from your description.**

Teachers' note This is a diagrammatic method of note-taking. As a further activity you could ask the children to take the same passages and underline key points. The children should write what they have discovered in their own words — not simply copy out what the book tells them.

Developing Literacy
Text Level Year 6
© A & C Black 2000

Skimming and scanning

When you skim a text, you read to gain a general impression.

When you scan a text, you read to find something specific.

- **Read the passage.**

In 1066 no one in Britain had a surname. When records such as the Domesday book started to be kept, it was important to distinguish between people with the same first name. A second name (a 'byname') was introduced and became the family name, handed down from father to son. The word 'surname' comes from the Latin 'supranomen', meaning 'an extra name'. By the fifteenth century, everybody had a surname.

- **Give the passage a title.** _____

- **Write down four important facts it tells you.**

    1. _____
    2. _____
    3. _____
    4. _____

- **Read these notes.**
- **Underline four key facts.**
- **Write questions about them.**

1. How did the surname 'Hughes' come about?

2. _____

3. _____

4. _____

> Surnames to 1400 – from various sources, e.g. from forenames called 'Christian' names (Hughes ⟋Hugh); from their families (Johnson ⟋son of John); from jobs (Smith ⟋black smith); from where people lived (Hill ⟋John by the hill – a kind of address); descriptions (Small).

Now try this!

- **Which did you find the easiest text from which to extract information? Why?**

Teachers' note This is an opportunity to link with other areas of the curriculum, such as history. This sheet enables the children to tackle difficult non-fiction texts by developing questions through 'skimming' and then 'scanning' the text in order to answer them.

Developing Literacy
Text Level Year 6
© A & C Black 2000

Writing a biography

When you write a biography, you write about someone else's life.

- Use this page to help you write notes about someone in your family.

Concentrate on interesting things and personal detail.

Name and age	Appearance	Job
Hobbies	Attitudes	Favourite possession
Favourite activities	Stories from the past	Plans for the future

Now try this!

- Use your notes to write a biography of your family member.

Teachers' note This is an opportunity for the children to carry out survey work by interviewing members of their family. The children could use a sheet for each person in their family.

Developing Literacy
Text Level Year 6
© A & C Black 2000

Writing an autobiography

- **Use this sheet to help you plan your** autobiography **. Use the first person 'I'.**

You could write about your family history to start with. Talk to people at home to help your research.

start here

You could go on to write about your parents or carers.

Where do you come into the story?

Write about the most important and memorable events in your life.

keep going!

- **Use your notes to write your** autobiography **.**
- **Where will you start? At the beginning? Or will you use a 'flashback' technique?**

Now try this!

Teachers' note Stress to the children that not every detail of their lives should be written down – only the moments which retain some significance. You could discuss how time will be structured in the narrative and where the autobiography should start for it to be most effective. Refer to page 31 (Flashbacks).

Developing Literacy
Text Level Year 6
© A & C Black 2000

A character's CV

Imagine you are a character in a book and you want to apply for a job.

- **Complete the form.**

A CV or 'curriculum vitae' is a list of the important details and events in someone's personal history.

Book title _____

Curriculum Vitae

Name: _____ Age: _____

Physical appearance: _____
_____

Education: _____
_____

Important events in your life: _____
_____
_____

Achievements: _____
_____

Qualities of character: _____
_____

Interests: _____
_____
_____

Relationships with others: _____
_____
_____

Other comments: _____
_____
_____

Now try this!

- **Write a character study using your notes.**

Teachers' note This work links closely with point of view and the representation of characters in another light. See also pages 55 and 56 for other ways for the children to use the details they have gathered about characters.

**Developing Literacy
Text Level Year 6
© A & C Black 2000**

A character's school report

- **Think of a character in a book.**
- **Write his or her school report.**

Design a school crest for the report.

Book title _____

School Report

Name: _____

Personal details: _____

_____

_____

Subject	Achievement	Teacher's comments

Qualities of character: _____

_____

Evidence: _____

_____

Other interests: _____

_____

How I see this person developing later in life:

_____

_____

_____

Now try this!

- **Explain how the character in the book came to behave in the way that he or she did.**

Teachers' note This sheet gives the children the opportunity to extract information about the character but also to infer what may have been responsible for the behaviour of the character. It is interesting to consider if characters in a story treat heroes/heroines differently from villains in childhood.

Developing Literacy
Text Level Year 6
© A & C Black 2000

A character's personal file

You are a private detective. You have followed a character you know from a book in order to write a report.

- Complete the notes.

Include evidence from the text.

CONFIDENTIAL

PRIVATE DETECTIVE'S PERSONAL FILE ON: _____

BOOK HE/SHE APPEARS IN: _____

AUTHOR: _____

What I saw the character say or do	Location/Other characters present	Conclusion about the character

MY SUMMARY: _____

_____

_____

_____

- Use your notes to write a character profile.
- Compare your views with those of a partner.

Now try this!

Teachers' note This activity encourages the children to focus on a character's words and actions and to draw conclusions from them. In the plenary section you could compare and discuss different children's conclusions about the same character. What evidence did they choose to prove their points?

**Developing Literacy
Text Level Year 6
© A & C Black 2000**

Be a journalist

- **Read the letter.**
- **Collect other views for and against the argument.**
- **Write a newspaper article on the subject.**
- **Follow the journalist's checklist.**

Dear Editor,
   I think fox-hunting should be banned for many reasons. The most obvious is that it is cruel. Humans would never let their cats or dogs be chased and killed like foxes are. So why should people be allowed to chase and kill these innocent creatures? Another reason why this so-called sport should be banned is that foxes are useful to farmers. They kill pests which destroy crops. Recent opinion polls show that seventy per cent of the population want a ban. It's time the government made up their mind. We should protest much more.

Lee Flemalone

Journalist's checklist

- Headline
- Introductory sentence
- Paragraph to explain introductory sentence
- Simple description
- Sub-headings
- Direct speech
- Reported speech
- Photograph

GOVERNMENT TOLD: MAKE UP YOUR MIND!

Continue on another piece of paper if necessary.

- **Produce your article on a word-processor, if possible, and set it out like a piece of journalism.**

Teachers' note Using a variety of newspapers as shared texts, you could ask the children to point out the relevant features of journalistic style (see page 43). The children could look more closely at the same piece of news from a variety of sources and discuss how language is being used.

Developing Literacy
Text Level Year 6
© A & C Black 2000

Using the Internet

- **Use this page to help you to research using the Internet.**

Subject of research: _____

Write the name of each site and its Internet address.

Most useful sites: _____
_____
_____
_____

What I found out: _____
_____
_____

- **Choose three sites. Answer ☑ or ☒.**

Write the site names at the top.

Was it easy to find the site?			
Was it easy to find your way around the site?			
Was there too much text?			
Was the text easy to read?			

- **Draw some conclusions.**

Good things about using the Internet for research: _____
_____
_____

Not so good things about using the Internet for research: _____
_____
_____

Now try this!

- **Write an explanation of how you used the Internet for your research.**

Teachers' note Explain to the children that they need to have a clear purpose in mind when using the Internet for research. To save time, they could keep useful sites in a 'favourites' folder.

Developing Literacy
Text Level Year 6
© A & C Black 2000

Writing effective arguments

- **Read the statements.**
- **Write on the chart the arguments for and against the subject.**

Add any other points you can think of.

Experiments on animals

- Polio vaccines developed by experiments on animals reduced the number of cases from 2,495 in 1958 (with 150 deaths) to 4 in 1975.
- There has been a 90% reduction in the death rate in children in the past 40 years. Experiments on animals played a vital part in developing the necessary treatments.
- It has been proved that animals are treated cruelly in laboratories.
- Moreover, much of this cruelty makes 'vanity' products such as cosmetics, not medicines.
- While people complain about experiments on animals, more than 400 million animals each year in Britain are killed to be eaten – about seven for each person.
- Cruelty is enabling big firms to make profits – the animals can't answer back. They are being taken advantage of.

Arguments for the subject	Arguments against the subject

Now try this!

- **Write a paragraph arguing for experiments on animals and a paragraph arguing against them. Use the statements from the chart.**

Teachers' note The most interesting arguments are often about the most controversial subjects, so allow the children to collect information to discuss such issues. Focus on the careful use of connectives which allow the argument to develop and move in different directions.

**Developing Literacy
Text Level Year 6
© A & C Black 2000**

Write a balanced report

- **Look at the diagram. Imagine you were standing at point X.**
- **Write a report for the police about what you saw.**

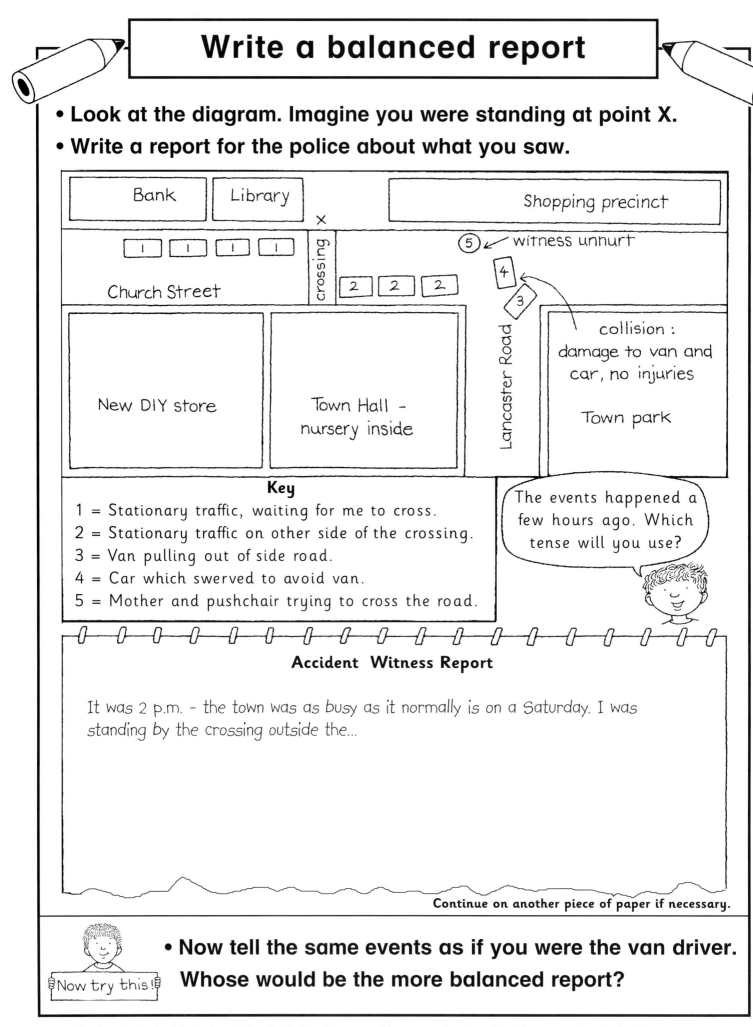

Bank Library

X

Shopping precinct

| 1 | 1 | 1 | 1 |

crossing

⑤ ← witness unhurt

4

3

Church Street

| 2 | 2 | 2 |

Lancaster Road

New DIY store

Town Hall - nursery inside

collision : damage to van and car, no injuries

Town park

Key

1 = Stationary traffic, waiting for me to cross.
2 = Stationary traffic on other side of the crossing.
3 = Van pulling out of side road.
4 = Car which swerved to avoid van.
5 = Mother and pushchair trying to cross the road.

The events happened a few hours ago. Which tense will you use?

Accident Witness Report

It was 2 p.m. - the town was as busy as it normally is on a Saturday. I was standing by the crossing outside the...

Continue on another piece of paper if necessary.

Now try this!

- **Now tell the same events as if you were the van driver. Whose would be the more balanced report?**

Teachers' note Explain to the children that when they are writing a report such as this, it is important to place the facts in the correct order. If the story were told from a different point of view, how 'balanced' would it be? This links with work on point of view (see page 9).

Developing Literacy
Text Level Year 6
© A & C Black 2000

Standard English

In this passage from *The Adventures of Tom Sawyer,*

Tom meets Huck at a haunted house. Huck is superstitious.

- **Read the passage.**

- **Underline the words and phrases that are not standard English.**

'Looky here, Tom, do you know what day it is?'

Tom mentally ran over the days of the week, and then quickly lifted his eyes with a startled look in them.

'My! I never once thought of it, Huck.'

'Well, I didn't neither, but all at once it popped on me that it was Friday.'

'Blame it; a body can't be too careful, Huck. We might 'a got into an awful scrape, tackling such things on a Friday.'

'Might! Better say we would! There's some lucky days maybe, but Friday ain't.'

'Any fool knows that. I don't reckon you was the first that found it out, Huck.'

'Well, I never said I was, did I? And Friday ain't all, neither. I had a rotten bad dream last night... dreamt about rats.'

'No! Sure sign of trouble. Did they fight?'

'No.'

'Well, that's good, Huck. But we'll drop this thing for to-day, and play. Do you know Robin Hood, Huck?'

'No. Who's Robin Hood?'

'I'll learn you,' said Tom.

FROM *The Adventures of Tom Sawyer*
BY MARK TWAIN

- **Re-write the passage in standard English.**

- **Which version gives you more sense of character?**

Now try this!

- **Write these phrases in standard English.**

1. He were the first.

2. I done it.

3. The book what she read.

4. I didn't neither.

5. You don't know nothing.

Teachers' note To introduce the activity, read the passage with the children noting how the language is that of real speech and hence is meant to give the reader a sense of the character of the two boys. The use of non-standard English is not 'wrong' as such but the children need to be aware of its appropriate use.

Developing Literacy
Text Level Year 6
© A & C Black 2000

Impersonal writing

- **Read these two texts. The sentences are in the wrong order.**
  The texts are written in | impersonal language | **.**
- **Where would you be likely to find these texts?** _____
  _____

- **Re-write the sentences in the correct order.**

A. To demonstrate water pressure

When the tape was removed, the water sprayed out through the holes. From this it is possible to see where the pressure is greatest.
First, a plastic bucket was taken.
Three holes were drilled in it – one near the rim, one in the centre and one near the base.
Then the bucket was filled with water.
The holes were sealed with masking tape.

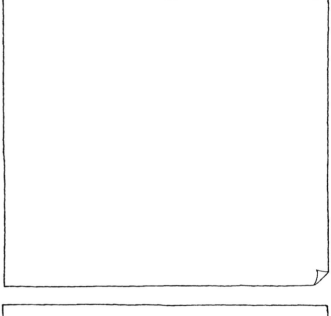

B. Growing crystals

This sugary liquid, called a solution, was placed in a beaker.
First, heated water was poured over sugar in a pan and stirred with a spatula until no more sugar would dissolve.
Crystals were seen to grow on the thread after a few days.
Then a sugar cube was tied with fine thread and suspended in the solution.

Now try this!

- **Circle the verbs in the passages. Which forms of verbs are used?** _____
- **Are pronouns such as 'I' or 'you' ever used?** _____
  Give a reason. _____

Teachers' note This work links with sentence-level work about the uses of verb forms, especially the active and the passive. You could ask the children to re-write the two passages using imperative verbs, 'Take a…', and using second person narration, 'You need… when you…'.

Developing Literacy
Text Level Year 6
© A & C Black 2000

Paragraphs

Paragraphs mark a new idea or style in
a piece of writing.

• Complete the plan with your ideas.

My favourite soap opera on TV:

Paragraph 1	The background – an introduction	_____
Paragraph 2	A summary of what the soap opera is about	_____
Paragraph 3	The characters	_____
Paragraph 4	One episode in detail to show its features	_____
Paragraph 5	Conclusion – how you hope the soap opera will develop	_____

Now try this!

• Use your notes to write your report in paragraphs.
• Try arranging the paragraphs in another order.
  Explain the differences when you do this.

Teachers' note Many children have difficulty knowing when to use new paragraphs. You could model with them through shared reading how new paragraphs occur when introducing new information or speakers, or when narrative is changing direction. (See the work on Flashbacks, page 31.)

Developing Literacy
Text Level Year 6
© A & C Black 2000

63

Text-types

- **Match the texts to their text-types.**

1. I never thought it was possible to enjoy Sports Day at school until the year my mum decided to enter the egg-and-spoon race.

An instructional text

An informational text

2. Take a 225g of flour and 175g of margarine. Rub in the fat with your fingers until the mixture looks like breadcrumbs. Add water to mix. Make sure the pastry is not sticky.

3. Did you know that the most conspicuous advertising sign was an electric sign for a French car manufacturer on the Eiffel Tower in Paris in 1925? It could be seen 25 miles away.

A persuasive text

A recount text

4. Unsightly hair on your legs? Well – we can solve all that. With NEW Swiss formula RIDOHAIR, your legs will be smooth and beautiful in seconds.

- **Complete the chart.**

Text	Text-type	Audience that it was written for
1.		
2.		
3.		
4.		

Now try this!

- **List the features of the style which helped you to identify each text-type.**

Think about:
- verb tenses
- language
- tone of voice.

Text-type	Features of style

Teachers' note In the plenary session you could discuss with the children for whom they think the passages were written and what the demands of that audience would be, for example: clear instructions to get things done, language to inform.

Developing Literacy
Text Level Year 6
© A & C Black 2000